FRIEND OF A FRIEND . . .

ALSO BY DAVID BURKUS

Under New Management:
How Leading Organizations Are
Upending Business as Usual

The Myths of Creativity:
The Truth About How Innovative Companies
and People Generate Great Ideas

FRIEND OF A FRIEND . . .

Understanding the Hidden Networks That Can Transform Your Life and Your Career

David Burkus

Houghton Mifflin Harcourt
Boston New York
2018

hmhco.com

Library of Congress Cataloging-in-Publication Data
Names: Burkus, David, (date) author.
Title: Friend of a friend . . . : understanding the hidden networks that can transform your life and your career / David Burkus.
Description: Boston : Houghton Mifflin Harcourt, 2018. | Includes bibliographical references and index.
Identifiers: LCCN 2017056986 (print) | LCCN 2017045593 (ebook) | ISBN 9780544971288 (ebook) | ISBN 9780544971264 (hardback)
Subjects: LCSH: Business networks. | BISAC: BUSINESS & ECONOMICS / Careers / General.
Classification: LCC HD69.S8 (print) | LCC HD69.S8 B8587 2018 (ebook) | DDC 650.1/3—dc23
LC record available at https://lccn.loc.gov/2017056986

Book design by Chrissy Kurpeski

Printed in the United States of America
DOC 10 9 8 7 6 5 4 3 2 1

To my parents

Contents

Introduction

Or
How I Learned to Stop Networking and Love Network Science

IN 1999, A YOUNG COMPUTER ENGINEER and aspiring entrepreneur named Adam Rifkin was looking for advice on his next move. In gathering advice, Rifkin sent an unsolicited email to a man he had never met in person named Graham Spencer. At the time, Spencer was one of the hottest names in the Silicon Valley tech community, having just completed the sale of his last start-up, Excite.com.[1]

Although Excite.com is still active, it's easy to forgive anyone who doesn't immediately recognize the name. In the age before Google and Facebook, however, Excite was one of the biggest brands on the Internet. Started in 1993 by Spencer and five of his friends, Excite had grown to become the front page of the Internet for a significant percentage of web-surfers. (This was back when people still used that term seriously.) Spencer and the Excite team had grown the website from a humble start-up to a vast collection of websites. They had some financial struggles, but the success of the website in drawing users eventually led them to a major payout. In early 1999, Excite was sold to the telecommunications company @Home for $6.7 billion. Needless to say, once the deal was finalized, Spencer was getting a lot of attention.

That Rifkin sent a cold email hoping for some advice from a Silicon Valley success story isn't unusual; who wouldn't at least try? What is unusual is that Spencer agreed to the request. Not only did Spencer volunteer to meet with Rifkin in person and answer any questions Rifkin had, but he went above and beyond that. Once Rifkin had explained his idea, Spencer connected Rifkin to a venture capitalist who became one of the first funders of the new start-up.

The overriding question is why, at the height of his popularity, and at the peak of the demand for his time, did Spencer agree to sit down with someone he had never met in person?

Because five years earlier, Rifkin and Spencer had built a webpage about punk rock bands.

More specifically, in 1994, as Rifkin was beginning his studies in computer science, he built a fan website dedicated to the emerging punk rock band Green Day. Despite it being the early days of the Internet, the website took off quickly. In fact, the website was getting so much attention that members of Green Day asked if they could take it over from Rifkin and make it their official website. Rifkin said yes. But Rifkin also received another request, from a young Graham Spencer, who felt that labeling Green Day as "punk rock" was taking attention away from "real" punk bands. So Rifkin and Spencer worked together and built a page on the Green Day website that listed other, lesser known bands. "A completely random set of events that happened in 1994 led to re-engaging with him over e-mails in 1999," Rifkin said. "Which led to my company getting founded in 2000."[2] Rifkin had helped Spencer, even though he could have ignored the request. Five years later, Spencer in turn helped Rifkin even though he too could have ignored the request.

While this story might seem exceptional, it's actually not that uncommon an occurrence for Rifkin. His career has been full of incidents of helping individuals who either were or would go on to be well-known figures in technology and business. Like the time Rifkin gave some contract work over to a young Ev Williams so he could keep afloat with a start-up called Blogger—which he later sold to Google for an undisclosed sum (though rumors estimate tens of millions). Williams would go on to start the company that would become Twitter. Or like the time Rifkin was starting another company and needed office space, and Reid Hoffman offered to let his team crash at LinkedIn until they got on their feet.[3]

Rifkin's story is filled with amazing anecdotes. He may not be a well-known name to everyone, but to the right people in his industry, he's more than well known. He's the best networker in the world. Literally. In 2011, *Fortune* magazine named Rifkin "the world's best networker"—since it turned out that he was more connected than anyone else to the most influential people on *Fortune*'s lists (Fortune 500, 40 Under 40, 50 Most Powerful Women, etc.).[4]

What is surprising about Rifkin earning this title isn't just that he is not the household name we would expect, but also that he doesn't fit the image of the world's best networker. He is not a tall, extroverted, dapper, energetic, eloquent, highly educated professional. "I am not an extrovert," he has said frequently. "Meeting people is not my favorite thing."[5] He describes himself as a little shy and awkward. He prefers a T-shirt and hoodie to a suit and tie. His look is often compared to a panda bear (a comparison he wears fairly proudly). He'd rather reconnect with old friends than work a room full of new people.

What Rifkin does have is *an understanding of how networks work*. Much of his initial strategy for building relationships and making connections wasn't gleaned from an advice book about being a power networker. It came from his graduate school work in computer science. "I feel fortunate to have learned networking from many excellent teachers," Rifkin once said. "And the greatest of these teachers was actually the Internet itself."[6] To Rifkin, human networks follow similar principles to computer networks. And studying those networks taught him several lessons about how to build and utilize better human networks. While we might think of our network as a collection of contact cards in a Rolodex (or more modernly, a collection of names in a contacts app), when Rifkin thought about networks, he saw them not as a collection of contacts but as the map of the connections between contacts. "A network is basically a set of people and the connections between those people," he explained.[7]

One lesson in particular was that computer networks grow in value as the number of nodes and the number of connections grow. (A similar lesson from network science, often referred to as Metcalfe's Law, is a mathematical expression of this idea.) "If you go about it the right way, then it's good for everyone," Rifkin explained. "If you go about it the wrong way, then it cuts off opportunities, not just for yourself but for others too."[8] So Rifkin committed himself to making introductions every single day. Eventually, he learned to scale his network building by building a whole community, 106 Miles, dedicated to keeping the tech community well connected. Today, 106 Miles has almost 10,000 members who interact regularly. It's a network unto itself. Although Rifkin isn't at the center of it anymore, it owes its existence to his perspective on networks and networking.

Rifkin's own extensive network, and the career success it has brought him, is more than an amazing story. It's a stern rejection of many of the misconceptions about what networking is and how it's supposed to work. One reason these misconceptions are widespread is that the majority of books, workshops, courses, speeches, and more on the subject are based on old and misguided advice. Specifically:

- *They say you should write and refine your "elevator pitch."*
- *They say you should never eat a meal alone.*
- *They say that you should repeat someone's name three times in the first few seconds of conversation (sometimes as advice for remembering the name, other times as a trick to get people to like you more).*
- *They will offer guidelines on how to work a room or how to meet new connections online.*

But all advice is autobiographical.[9] Advice, even advice about networks, represents little more than one person's single story projected onto others. Advice, at its core, says, "I did this and it worked, so you should do it too," or the slightly more convincing, "I wasn't doing this, but then I did and it changed my life." As well meaning, inspirational, and accurate as another person's autobiography might be, it's still one person, with one specific set of skills, one personality, in one specific location, at one specific time. So what if you're not that person with that personality at that point in life? What if you're not the tall, extroverted, dapper, energetic, eloquent, highly educated professional who's giving you the advice? Would it still work for you? Would you even want to try it?

Many people report feeling sketchy or even dirty when they engage in or think about networking. We think about the creepy salesman at the last networking mixer we attended, the one who sped around the room handing out business cards like candy and always scanning for people more "important" than us to talk to. Or we think about that old classmate who just hit the job market unexpectedly and has started frantically emailing everyone in her address book, blanketing LinkedIn with connection requests, and asking just about everyone out for coffee and a "quick chat." Networking seems to many of us to be an insincere way to manipulate relationships for personal gain. This is the repulsive stereotype most people have of networkers, and it's no surprise that it is not a pleasant picture.

In one study, the researchers Tiziana Casciaro, Francesca Gino, and Maryam Kouchaki found that even just thinking about networking leaves most people feeling dirty . . . literally dirty.[10] In one round of the study, the researchers asked 306 adults to remember a time when they reached out to form a new relationship. One group was asked to imagine a time when they sought out professional contacts who could help their career (what the researchers called "instrumental networking"). Another group was asked to imagine a time when they reached out to someone in their industry to form a personal connection, without consideration of professional gain (what the researchers called "personal networking" but we could also label "being a decent human being").

Afterwards, participants in both groups were asked to perform a word completion task and given word fragments (such as "S _ _ P" or "W _ _ H") that could be filled in to spell seemingly random words ("STEP" or "WISH") or words related to cleanliness ("SOAP" or "WASH"). It has been well demonstrated in previous research that feeling morally tainted increases our desire for cleanliness and that desire manifests in subtle shifts in cognition—including how we do a word completion task. Unsurprisingly, Casciaro and her colleagues found that those in the instrumental networking group—those who had to imagine a time when they played the role of the stereotypical networker—completed the task with words related to cleanliness. The implication is that the act of networking made them feel morally tainted and literally dirty.

In a follow-up round, the researchers took the experiment online. They asked students to think of a time when they had reached out to get to know someone better. One group of students was asked about social connections and the other about professional relationships. The researchers then asked the social group to reach out to the person they were thinking of via Facebook (a social media website mainly used to build and maintain friendships), and the professional group was asked to reach out to the person they had remembered via LinkedIn (a social media website mainly used to build and maintain professional relationships). Afterwards, all students were surveyed about how they were feeling. Again, the professional relationships group reported feeling physically dirtier than those in the social relationships group.

Despite these results, Casciaro and her colleagues also found that networking was hugely important. In a different study, they surveyed hundreds of lawyers throughout North America and asked them how frequently they engaged in networking. They found that those who engaged in making new connections and strengthening old ones were better performers (in terms of billable hours and hence compensation) than those who didn't. Their findings align with a significant body of research that demonstrates that networking—making and strengthening connections to others—is vitally important for professional success. Likewise, understanding how the networks inside an organization truly operate dramatically improves its overall importance.

But what do you get when you combine an understanding that networks and relationships are important with the commonly shared belief that networking activities are awkward and dirty? You get perhaps the most commonly expressed maxim about networking: "It's not what you know; it's who you know."

This phrase is a curious one. People have written it down or spoken it aloud for at least seven decades (and probably more than that),[11] but usually just to express exasperation. "I didn't get the job [the sale/the promotion] because I didn't have the right connections." You may have even said it yourself at some point—in a moment of similar frustration. If success is mostly a matter of who you know, then we start to believe that we only have two choices: settle for less, or adopt the stereotypical networking prowler.

But what if there is another choice?

In fact, there is.

Researchers Rob Cross and Robert Thomas have found time and again that "who you know" is important, but just knowing lots of people won't get you there. "In fact, we've found that individuals who simply know a lot of people are less likely to achieve standout performance," they write. "Political animals with lots of connections to corporate and industry leaders don't win the day, either."[12] Collecting contacts isn't the surefire route to success.

In light of this research showing that it's not necessarily about who you know, perhaps another commonly used phrase is more accurate: it's about knowing who is a "friend of a friend." It's about getting a full picture of the network you already have access to, and learning how to improve it.

Like Adam Rifkin, understanding how networks work, how to navigate them, and how to tend to the community they represent is what determines a lot of your career success and a lot of organizations' ability to perform. Knowing who your friends are and who *their* friends are, so you can gain a better understanding of the community, will lead to better odds that your network will enhance your success.

Fortunately, this insight is backed up by decades of research from the worlds of sociology and network science. This research supports that being connected to a strong network provides major advantages—access to diverse skills and perspectives, the ability to learn private information, and the type of expertise and influence that makes it easier to attain power—which sociologists refer to as *social capital*. An intriguing term that appears to have been invented by six different people at six different times, social capital takes its definition opposite *physical capital*—financial resources, inventory, property, and the like.[13] Just as those things have value, sociologists argue, so do the connections and networks of our social capital—especially when we know how to leverage that capital. In one study, led by the renowned sociologist Ronald Burt (more on him soon), it was found that educating executives about network structures and principles led to dramatic improvements in performance.[14] Those who took the training were 36 to 42 percent more likely to improve their performance than similarly qualified but untrained peers, and 42 to 74 percent more likely to be promoted.

And that is what this book is about.

This isn't just a book about networking. It's not like any networking book you have read (or ignored) before. This is a book about how networks actually work. This isn't another collection of rote advice and specific instructions on how to meet new people or how to work a room. It's not a manual for managing your social media and online presence. There are plenty of those guides already and adding one more wouldn't help—especially because just collecting contacts doesn't work. Instead, this is a book that takes a deep dive into the proven science of networks and shares the implications for anyone looking to upgrade their connections and relationships.

I won't be sharing anecdotal advice from stereotypical networkers; instead, we will examine real case studies of people and companies who found success because they found (knowingly or not) a strategy in line with the research.

Knowing how networks come together is the secret weapon behind a powerful networking strategy. It works better than the entire collection of tools.

And that is where we are headed.

The next chapter explains the types of network connections that are most likely to provide you with new information and opportunities (and a quick hint: it's probably not who you tend to interact with the most). After that, chapter 2 examines an old party game and reveals the clues it holds to just how large and useful your total network really is. Chapter 3 deals with your networking strategy: is it better to try to connect with everyone in one industry or profession, or is it better to be the connector between these groups? Chapter 4 answers the common call to break down silos with a reminder that sometimes staying in your silo can have tremendous benefits—it just depends on how often you're there. Chapter 5 examines how your network affects the teams you rely on, and explains why part of cultivating a high-performing network is being willing to decrease or cut off how frequently you interact with some connections. Chapter 6 describes just how large your network can become, and how above-average networkers really do have above-average networks. Chapter 7 looks at the implications of above-average networks for your own plan: will it always be an uphill battle and a constant process to make key connections, or can you grow your network passively?

Then we turn to some of the more surprising findings from network science that will have you reevaluating your entire network. Chapter 8 describes an intriguing quirk of social networks: it is possible to appear more popular and connected than you really are—but is it worthwhile? Chapter 9 issues a dire warning for anyone building their network: more isn't better if it means more of the same. Chapter 10 reveals the solution to this dilemma, showing that *where* and *how* you make new connections affect how valuable they will become. Chapter 11, the final chapter, moves away from the entire network to look at individual connections, revealing that part of who you know includes how (and how well) you know them.

In addition to the implications for individuals, the findings from network science carry implications for how leaders shape their organizations and how companies try to market their brands through customer networks. When relevant, these will be explored as well.

To help you move from ideas to action, or from scientific research to practice, each chapter ends with an activity you can do quickly that will help you either better understand your current network or take the first steps to strengthening it. In addition, we examine the role of online tools and social media services in building and maintaining your network and show you when those tools might actually become counterproductive—which happens more often than you might think, since online tools only seem to work well when they reinforce off-line principles of human connection. (Perhaps that is why studies are showing that the more time individuals spend with online-only connections the more lonely they report feeling. Also, as people increase their use of online tools, their sense of social isolation seems to increase as well.[15])

Your connections matter. But so does how you know them, why you know them, where you met them, and who else they know. All of these elements are explained by the network around you—all your friends of friends.

By the end of this book, I hope you have become more effective at making and strengthening the key connections that will change your work and career. But I hope you do that not by just taking advice. Rather, I hope you become more effective because you've learned how the network around you works—and how to work it.

— 1 —

FIND STRENGTH IN WEAK TIES

Or
Why Your Old Friends Are Better Than Your New Friends

We tend to act as if our closest friends are our biggest assets. While that may be true for social support or for trusted information, it's not so true when it comes to opportunity. Research shows that our biggest opportunities and best sources of new information actually come from our "weak ties" or "dormant ties" — our connections with people we don't see often or haven't spoken to in a long time. This means that if we want to learn something new or make a job change, reaching out to our old friends is a better move than keeping it "just between friends" by connecting only with the people we're closest to now.

LORENZO FERTITTA NEVER PLANNED ON disrupting the prizefighting industry or on saving the sport of mixed martial arts (MMA) from regulatory extinction.

The son of casino magnate Frank Fertitta Jr., Lorenzo was no stranger to the world of combat sports, but his future was almost certainly going to be in the casino industry. However, because of an old and distant high school friend, he has spent the better part of the last two decades turning the once-crippled Ultimate Fighting Championship (UFC) franchise into a worldwide brand valued at more than $4 billion. But Lorenzo Fertitta isn't even the lead actor in the story. That title goes to Dana White, for reactivating a weak tie in his network that dramatically enhanced both his and Lorenzo Fertitta's net worth.

From the outside looking in, White and Fertitta resemble and act like lifelong friends on a journey to continuously grow the UFC and the sport of MMA. But their deep friendship is actually relatively new. They attended the same high school, Bishop Gorman, a Roman Catholic preparatory school in Las Vegas, Nevada, and tended to associate with the same circles of friends, but they themselves rarely interacted. "We had a lot more in common after school than in school," said White. "I got kicked out of Gorman twice. Lorenzo was the role model: A-student, football player, going on to college and college after college."[1]

White was correct. Lorenzo Fertitta went on to the University of San Diego and then earned an MBA from New York University. After school, Fertitta partnered with his brother, Frank III, first by starting a business renting pay phones and slot machines, then buying real estate on the outskirts of Las Vegas, and finally merging their company with their father's chain of casinos and taking the new entity public.

As for White, after he got kicked out of Bishop Gorman not once but twice, his parents sent him to Maine to live with his grandmother. White finished high school there and actually spent some time at college, but did not graduate. He floated through a variety of different jobs, everything from a bellhop to a boxing trainer. Eventually, he moved back to Las Vegas and started a gym. Then he started two more. Eventually, White found himself managing the careers of two fighters, Tito Ortiz and Chuck

Liddell, as they competed in the UFC. It would be nearly a decade after White left Bishop Gorman before he talked to either of the Fertitta brothers again.[2]

When they did, it was back in Las Vegas, and it was the result of a chance encounter at the wedding of a mutual friend from high school. Dana and Lorenzo quickly bonded over their mutual love of combat sports. White's passion for MMA quickly turned both of the Fertitta brothers into new fans. Lorenzo Fertitta was already serving on the Nevada State Athletic Commission, which regulated all combat sports in that state. Perhaps most notably, he was a commissioner when Mike Tyson bit off Evander Holyfield's ear. "I was one of the guys who had to tell Mike to pack up and go," Lorenzo Fertitta said.[3] It was a time when all combat sports, especially MMA, were being highlighted for their brutality.

As for the UFC, it was fighting hard just to stay alive and in business. Senator John McCain was leading the charge to ban MMA and even referred to it as "human cockfighting." One by one, each state and state athletic commission began to outlaw the sport, forcing the UFC to become creative in how it staged its events. Eventually, it lost its pay-per-view distribution, which meant ticket sales at live shows had to serve as the main source of revenue.

Through his work managing fighters, White learned that the UFC's original owners were tired of putting up a fight and were looking to sell their franchise. So White reached out to his long-lost friend Lorenzo Fertitta. Within a month, the Fertitta brothers had purchased the UFC for $2 million, using private funds. "It was probably the worst brand in the United States because of all the negativity around it," Lorenzo Fertitta said. The brothers did not even have the blessing of their father. "Dad was a fairly conservative guy," said Frank Fertitta. "He asked us not to do it. I think that's the only time that Lorenzo and I actually went against what he wanted us to do. Thank God we did."[4]

Little by little, White and the Fertittas grew the struggling league from backwater shows to sold-out arenas and millions of television viewers. The Fertitta brothers knew that the sport would not survive without regulatory approval. Fortunately, Lorenzo's connections with the athletic commissions helped him understand and work toward the changes they would need to make to get that approval. They added a new rule structure, established weight classes, and by some accounts made it a safer sport for participants than boxing. White's experience with the fighters they inherited no doubt made those changes an easier sell to the athletes themselves.

All this being said, their first big event was, by most accounts, a disaster. It was disorganized and ran over time, so the pay-per-view broadcast was cut short before the main event.[5] However, the Fertittas continued to put more effort and money (over $40 million) into the venture. In 2004, they gambled even bigger. One of the Fertittas' casinos, Green Valley Ranch, had played host to a reality show on the Discovery Channel, and the brothers thought a similar venture might help raise awareness of their fight league.[6] They pitched a show where aspiring young fighters were shown living and training together, all the while competing for a contract with the UFC. The show was turned down by every network except Spike TV, which agreed to air it if the Fertittas paid the $10 million production cost themselves.

The show was a hit almost from the beginning and rapidly increased the fan base for mixed martial arts. It also made Dana White into a television star, showcasing his brash style, his understanding of what it means to be a fighter, and his knowledge of what it takes to be a champion. The show has now run for over twenty seasons and continues to recruit new fans to the sport. By 2005, the Fertittas had recouped their original investments in the UFC.[7] Senator McCain has even changed his tune, if only slightly. "They haven't made me a fan, but they have made progress," he said in a 2007 interview on National Public Radio.[8]

As part of the purchase, the Fertittas maintained an equal ownership of the enterprise, something their lawyers were not happy about.[9] Legal counsel wanted a way to resolve disputes in case of a stalemate. They solved that in two ways. First, White was given a 10 percent stake in the organization and tasked with running the day-to-day operations. Second, they added a clause in their ownership contract that all disputes between the brothers would be settled with a jiujitsu match, with White playing the role of referee. "It hasn't happened yet," Lorenzo Fertitta joked.[10] The two brothers and White have a great relationship. They work out together regularly and communicate frequently. "We both bring something very different to the table, but at the end of the day, we've got a great dynamic," Lorenzo Fertitta said.[11]

In 2011, the UFC signed a seven-year broadcasting deal with the FOX Sports Media Group valued at $700 million.[12] The company produces more than forty live events every year and is broadcast in more than 1 billion households around the world. In 2013, Dana White was named the "sports innovator of the year" for his role in the turnaround.[13] And in 2016, the Fertittas and White successfully sold the UFC for $4 billion to a group of private investors, including the William Morris Endeavor Agency, Silver Lake Partners, KKR, and MSD Capital (the investment firm of the technology billionaire Michael Dell). "It's the largest deal ever in the history of sports," Lorenzo Fertitta said at the time.[14] He is not far off. In terms of sports, it is twice what Steve Ballmer paid in 2014 to purchase the Los Angeles Clippers. In terms of all entertainment, $4 billion rivals what the Walt Disney

Company paid George Lucas for the entire Star Wars franchise in 2012, which was hailed as the "deal of the century" when it happened.[15] For his part, White's personal payout was reported to be more than $350 million.[16] Pretty good payday for a former bellhop and boxing trainer.

Whatever measure is used, the story of the UFC is one about a remarkable transition from the brink of collapse to a multibillion-dollar valuation. And none of it would have happened without a chance meeting of two former classmates.

The Forgotten Network

White and Fertitta's chance interaction at that wedding may seem like a fluke, but it is actually a textbook case of how the forgotten parts of our network yield bigger opportunities than most of us realize. Their relationship at the time resembled what sociologists refer to as *weak ties*—people we maintain a connection with but rarely interact with. By contrast, *strong ties* are the connections we regularly return to—those friends and coworkers we feel comfortable around because we know, like, and trust them.

Our tendency when things get tough is to seek out trusted, familiar counsel. When we need a new job, for example, we default to those close to our network. We tell our friends and family, then skip over our weak ties, ironically, and go right to coldly responding to job postings online. Or when we need advice about a major problem, we tend to share our dilemma only with those close to us—those we feel comfortable around. But that comfort comes at a cost. Most of the strong ties in our network are connected to each other. They are often so tightly clustered that information known by one person is already known by everyone in that cluster. In contrast, our weak ties often build a bridge from one cluster to another and thus give us access to new information. Even though the strong ties in our life are more likely to be motivated to help us, it turns out that our weak ties' access to new sources of information may be more valuable than our strong ties' motivation.

Consider how Dana White's strong ties were already in the UFC world, while Lorenzo Fertitta's network gave him access to casinos to put on events and the connections to the athletic commission needed to change attitudes toward the sport. White found himself inside a community of individuals who knew their sport was dying but couldn't find a way to revive it; Fertitta was in a different community of Las Vegas entertainers who mostly focused on boxing. White had the knowledge of MMA; Lorenzo Fertitta had the knowledge of how to get the sport regulated and marketed like boxing. Their chance meeting at a friend's wedding connected these two seemingly distant clusters and unlocked an extremely valuable solution.

This counterintuitive finding first came from a now-classic study by the sociologist Mark Granovetter. In 1970, as a PhD student at Harvard University, Granovetter decided to conduct a study of job transitions. When surveying respondents, he would often ask whether a friend had told them about their current job. Respondents would often answer with something like: "Not a friend, but an acquaintance," which suggested to Granovetter that he ought to look further.[17] In the end, he surveyed hundreds of professional, technical, and managerial job-changers living in the suburbs of Boston, asking them about the contacts who had told them about the job opportunity they ended up applying for and accepting.

Specifically, he asked how often they were seeing those contacts around the time they received the job information. Granovetter used three categories: often (at least twice a week), occasionally (more than once a year but less than twice a week), and rarely (once a year or less). When Granovetter looked at the collected results, he found that fewer than 17 percent of job-changers saw their contacts often. Over 55 percent said they saw their contact occasionally, and over 27 percent said they rarely saw this person.

While between once a year and less than twice a week is admittedly a large margin, it's very representative of the variance in contact most of us maintain with our weaker relationships. Weak ties are those colleagues we don't plan to see, but when we do it's easy to catch up quickly. "The skew is clearly to the weak end of the continuum," Granovetter wrote in his 1973 paper presenting this data.[18] That paper, "The Strength of Weak Ties," would go on to become one of the most cited papers in sociology.

Granovetter's surprising findings run opposite to what most of us do when faced with a problem to solve, a choice to make, or the sudden need to find a job. It makes sense to share your situation with friends, family members, and trusted colleagues. They know you best and are most interested in helping you. But, as Granovetter found, the odds that they have any useful information or leads that you don't already have are slim. Moreover, the odds that everyone in your close circle will offer the same information or advice are great—our closest contacts tend to share the same contacts as us. Our weak ties are irregular contacts precisely because they tend to operate in different social circles. They interact with people different from our inner circle and learn different information. As a result, *weak ties become our best source for the new information that we need to resolve our dilemmas*.

Weak ties are stronger sources of information not just about job opportunities. Granovetter's work inspired researchers to study the other ways in which weak ties bring us new and valuable information and opportunities. Martin Ruef, a professor at Duke University, studied how entrepreneurs rely on strong and weak ties and the effects on their ability to be innovative.[19] Ruef surveyed more than 700 entrepreneurial teams who were launching new businesses and gathered data on the sources of their ideas, the structure of their team, the advisers or partners they sought, their patent applications, and the novelty of their business ideas. In particular, he was looking at the strength of the connections between the source of the teams' business ideas and the innovativeness of those ideas. To judge the strength of connections, he asked participants to classify the source of their business idea as: (1) coming from discussions with family and friends (strong ties); (2) coming from discussions with business associates, customers, or suppliers (weak ties); or (3) coming from observing discussions in the media, in the industry, or among existing competitors (what he called *directed ties,* since the information flow was only in one direction). To assess innovation, Ruef used two measures: patent and trademark applications as an objective measurement, and a subjective comparison of the teams' ideas against long-standing research on the categories of innovation.

When Ruef tabulated the results, he found that those teams whose business ideas came from discussions with weak ties were more innovative as judged by both measures. The fact that they sought more patent and trademark applications meant their ideas were likely more original and hence called for intellectual property protection. And their business idea was stronger across the categories of innovation, meaning the business model itself was more innovative than those businesses started by teams relying on strong ties. "Weak ties allow for more experimentation in combining ideas from disparate sources and impose fewer demands for social conformity than do strong ties," Ruef said.[20]

Taken together, Ruef's findings are consistent with the

strength of weak ties phenomenon first discovered by Granovetter. Just as the weak ties of job hunters are more likely to provide novel information about job opportunities, the weak ties of entrepreneurs are more likely to provide a novel perspective or discovery that can yield an idea for a new business. Similarly, while job hunters relying on strong ties have to endure the steep challenge, while unemployed, of convincing potential employers to make an offer, entrepreneurs relying on strong ties have to endure the difficult path of differentiating their business from the crowd. "Our results suggest that entrepreneurs can avoid the pitfalls of conformity by diversifying their networks," Ruef wrote of his findings.[21]

The research clearly supports the idea that in order to develop the most diverse information and create the most opportunity, we need to move beyond our strong ties and gain the fresh perspectives of our weaker connections. But not all weak ties are created equally. Strong ties may be more motivated to help us by bonds of familiarity and trust, but there is one form of weak ties with almost as much goodwill toward us while still offering new information: weak ties that used to be stronger. Even in Granovetter's original study, he noticed the role that former colleagues and long-lost friends played in helping individuals. "Chance meetings or mutual friends operated to reactivate such ties," Granovetter noted. "It is remarkable that people receive crucial information from individuals whose very existence they have forgotten."[22] Over time, other researchers would come up with a shorter name for such a weak tie that used to be stronger. They would label it a *dormant tie,* and their research would prove just how valuable these weak connections are.

The researchers Daniel Levin, Jorge Walter, and Keith Murnighan have been studying the power of dormant ties for almost a decade. Specifically, they have been surveying business executives, encouraging them to deliberately reactivate old connections and then observing the results. And the results have been quite powerful. In one experiment, the trio asked a group of 224 executives from four executive MBA classes to reconnect with two people to whom they had not spoken for at least three years, but who they thought would have advice that would help them on a major work project.[23] Specifically, the executives were to contact one person with whom they had shared a strong relationship before they fell out of touch, and also one individual with whom they had a weak tie relationship. In addition, the executives selected two current contacts (one strong, one weak) from whom they had already sought advice during the course of their project. The researchers then asked executives to assess all four contacts' advice in terms of value (actionable knowledge), novelty, trust, and the extent to which they had a shared perspective.

As you can imagine, many of these executives were not excited about the idea of cold-calling old colleagues and asking for advice. However, as the researchers and the executives themselves discovered, these old colleagues ended up becoming a tremendous resource. In short, the advice from the dormant ties was more likely to be valuable than the advice from current connections. Likewise, the dormant ties were more likely to provide unexpected insights and more novel advice than current ties. "In spite of their initial hesitation," Levin, Walter, and Murnighan wrote, "almost all of the executives in our studies report that they have received tremendous value from reconnecting their dormant relationships."[24]

The researchers weren't satisfied yet, however. It was still possible that one of the reasons dormant ties provided so much value was simply that they were top of mind when the executives were asked to think of old colleagues whose information would be useful. Most of us have more dormant ties than current ones, after all, so the probability is pretty high that the most useful counsel on a project would come from the larger pool of old colleagues. So the researchers tested a separate group of over 100 executives drawn from the same programs and gave them a different task. Instead of just selecting two dormant ties, these executives were asked to make a list of ten possible people to reconnect with and then rank them based on perceived usefulness. The executives were then told to reconnect with their top choice and with another person on the list chosen at random. After both conversations, the researchers measured the value of the advice in the same way as in the first study. "We originally thought that usefulness would drop off as people went down their list," the researchers wrote. "But the data did not show that."[25] Instead, the value of the advice tended to be consistent no matter what the executives' preconceived notions were. This suggests that the benefits of dormant ties have more to do with the dormancy of the ties themselves than with the perceived expertise.

The research on dormant ties reveals three main reasons for their strength. First, like weak ties, dormant ties can hold a wealth of new, different, and unexpected insights. Just because we have lost touch with someone doesn't mean that person has become extinct. Instead, our dormant ties are still around and interacting with other social circles and having new experiences. Second, reaching out to dormant ties specifically for advice is efficient; the contact with them is often much quicker than conversations with current colleagues who might be collaborating on multiple projects. And third, because many dormant ties, unlike weak ties, were once stronger relationships, their trust and motivation to help are much stronger than is true for current weak ties.

While dormant ties have been proven to be a great source of new insights and also to be a stronger form of weak ties, the truth is that not all dormant ties are equal. We all have someone we have lost touch with for a very specific reason. Levin, Walter, and Murnighan found that predicting which dormant ties would have the most valuable insights was so difficult that it inspired them to look even further into which dormant ties tend to be the most valuable.

In a follow-up study, the researchers repeated their method of surveying over 100 executives and asking them to reconnect with old contacts.[26] As in the previous experiment, they asked the executives to recall ten old contacts and to rank them by preference. Also as before, the executives were then asked to reach out to their most preferred contact and one other contact randomly chosen from their list of ten. However, unlike the previous study, this one included a survey of the executives before contact was made. The researchers asked the executives how briefly they had known their old contacts, how frequently or infrequently they had communicated with them before the relationship went dormant, and also how each old contact's status or organizational rank compared to the executive's own. All of the executives were also asked for their expectations about the trustworthiness and willingness to help of each of their contacts.

Then, after the executives reconnected either in person or via phone, the researchers followed up and asked a series of questions about the value of the advice received, as well as the novelty of the ideas and the levels of trust and shared perspective experienced. Surprisingly, when examining the results, the researchers found that executives consistently rated the advice from their more infrequent connections as more novel and useful . . . but also that the executives generally preferred to reconnect with people they saw as being more familiar. In other words, when reactivating dormant ties, the weaker dormant ties gave much better advice when reactivated, but those were also the exact type of dormant ties that most executives preferred to avoid. "Our executives displayed a strong bias to choose potential reconnections that turned out not to be the most valuable," the researchers wrote.[27] Despite this bias, preference didn't show much of an effect on the assessment of the conversation itself—almost all of the executives said they enjoyed and benefited from all conversations regardless of prior preference.

These findings suggest that, even among dormant ties, weaker connections are a more novel, valuable, and useful resource, which means Granovetter's strength of weak ties phenomenon applies even among old colleagues. Taken altogether, the strength of weaker ties runs counter to a lot of our preferences and even some conventional networking beliefs.

Like the executives in the study, most of us prefer to keep our conversations and advice-seeking inside a small, trusted circle of colleagues, despite solid evidence that the novelty of the information that this tight cluster can provide is severely limited. Even when forced to reconnect with dormant ties, we may tend to stay safe and to reconnect with those individuals with whom we are more familiar and who are less likely to provide the benefit of new intel.

At the other end of the networking spectrum, much of the conventional networking advice is focused on reaching out and meeting brand-new people. While that is a noble goal in and of itself, and new connections are likely to provide novel and valuable information and opportunities, the research from Levin, Walter, and Murnighan encourages us to consider old, dormant ties in our network before spending so much energy investing in new relationships. After all, dormant ties are almost as likely to give us great counsel, and they will do so much more efficiently, since reactivating an old connection is much faster than building a brand-new relationship from scratch.

New Ideas from Old Connections

It was this exact situation—the challenge of building new relationships and the ease of reactivating old ones—that Scott Harrison faced when he decided to start a new nonprofit organization. And it was the novelty that his dormant ties provided that led Harrison to revolutionize the way in which the nonprofit world operates. Before Harrison was the founder and face of charity: water, he was a young teenager rebelling against his upbringing and building a life as a nightclub promoter in New York City. After growing up in New Jersey in a household with a strong Christian ethos, Harrison fled to the big city to study at New York University. By his own admission, he wasn't exactly the ideal student, but he did learn how to throw a great party.

After graduation, Harrison found work as a promoter in New York's nightclub scene. He would organize parties for clubs, fashion magazines, and alcohol brands. And he was good at it. Eventually, corporate brands began sponsoring not just his parties but Harrison himself. He was paid to go out in public and drink certain brands of alcohol and wear certain brands of clothing. And he had also mastered the art of nonchalantly facing a logo or label toward any nearby cameras. His success and fame brought him a great deal of contacts. At one point he had 15,000 names in his address book. This wealth of connections and his ability to throw great parties earned Harrison a lot of money, but it also left him pretty miserable. "I had a Rolex, a grand piano, an apartment, a Labrador retriever," Harrison reflected, "and I came face to face with what a scumbag I was."[28]

Desperate to make a deep and personal change, Harrison decided to pursue a life of service. He blindly reached out to a variety of humanitarian organizations but was turned down by every group except one—presumably, his party animal back story was too hard to hide.

So with no other options, Harrison joined the crew of a Mercy Ships expedition to Liberia. The ship was a floating hospital where medical professionals volunteered their time to bring free medicine and surgical procedures to the world's poorest communities. "The chief medical officer was a surgeon who left Los Angeles to volunteer for two weeks—23 years ago," Harrison recalled.[29]

For his part, Harrison had convinced the staff of the organization that he was a photojournalist, and so his job became to use a camera lens to document the extreme poverty and dramatic transformations he witnessed. For the first time, Harrison saw just how severe the problem was. He met families who lived on less money per year than what he used to sell bottles of vodka for. "I was utterly astonished at the poverty that came into focus through my camera lens. Often through tears, I documented life and human suffering I'd thought unimaginable," Harrison said.[30] Initially, he had signed on for an eight-month expedition. He stayed with Mercy Ships for two years. "There was really no going back after my third day."[31]

During those two years, Harrison also saw the primary cause of a lot of suffering and left motivated to find a solution. "Of all of the issues I had seen facing the poor, water seemed to be the root cause," Harrison said.[32] "It was responsible for 80 percent of all disease. Water and lack of sanitation were responsible for 80 percent of all sickness on the planet, and there are a billion people without it." He was resolved to find a way to solve this problem—to bring clean water to every person who needed it. A big enough goal by itself, it was made almost insurmountable by his lack of connections to anyone involved in combating the water crisis. Harrison had learned from being seriously rebuffed when he tried to blindly reach out to humanitarian organizations in the past. Now, instead of forcing his way in and working to make new connections, he decided to reactivate his dormant ties. "It dawned on me what an opportunity it would be if my previous contacts could be corralled to make a difference," Harrison said.[33]

He went back to his old nightclub and fashion colleagues, most of whom he hadn't spoken to since sailing for Liberia two years prior. He started small at first, but then gathered momentum. Given where his dormant ties were, his first project was actually a party, his own thirty-first birthday party. He leveraged his old colleagues to book a nightclub so trendy that it hadn't yet opened to the public and invited almost his entire contact list. "As people walked into the nightclub, they walked past images of people drinking dirty water. Then those images turned to images of drillers, and then they turned to people drinking clean water," Harrison explained. "I asked everybody to pay on the way in and 100 percent of the money would go to our first projects in Uganda."[34] Seven hundred people attended the party.

After the party, things started to move quickly, but not in the direction of traditional philanthropy. Harrison followed up with his contacts, whom he knew would be concerned about how the donated money was spent. "I was with people who weren't giving to charities. So I was forced to try to create a business model that would resonate with them," he explained.[35] To do this, Harrison had pictures taken of the wells that were dug and emailed them out to everyone who attended the party. The response was incredible. "Half of them couldn't even remember being at the party but they were blown away by the pictures and the difference they had made," he said.[36] In effect, Harrison had found a new community of people interested in and willing to contribute to charity, but to whom the traditional models didn't appeal.

From that party onward, charity: water committed to a new model, one where 100 percent of individual donations would be directly used to provide access to clean water. In addition, everyone who donated would be kept informed on the group's progress and the end results of their donations. To do this, Harrison and his growing team established two bank accounts from the beginning: one for donations from a small group of trusted donors who had committed to paying the overhead, and the other for the majority of donations from individuals who, like his dormant ties from the fashion and nightclub world, wanted to know their money was going right to the project. While a few foundations and trusts work this way, almost all were established through a gift from one or two major donors—billionaires who decided to give away some of their wealth by starting a foundation. The idea of someone who was not a billionaire starting from scratch and building a nonprofit organization that functioned similar to a charitable trust was unheard of. The rest of the philanthropic world just didn't work that way. "Nobody had ever done our model before," Harrison recalled.[37] And perhaps he wouldn't have done it either had he tried to network and make new contacts in that world. Instead, it was his weak ties that led him to a very different idea about how to run a charity.

His old contacts also helped him think differently about raising awareness. From the beginning, charity: water put a special emphasis on storytelling and great design, the same elements it takes to run a profitable fashion brand or to put together a remarkable event. "I think the second thing we did was take over New York City parks," Harrison said.[38] And by "take over" he really does mean take over—his team made it almost impossible for any passing New Yorkers to avoid the issue of the water crisis. They took a series of striking photos that captured the needs and efforts of impoverished communities that needed access to clean water and plastered these images onto large tanks of dirty pond water, forcing passersby to imagine what it would be like if they faced the same daily challenge of finding clean drinking water. The exhibit worked, drawing out tens of thousands of people and raising tens of thousands of dollars for the cause.

It also led a lot of people to look up charity: water online and encouraged them to join what would become their most important fund-raiser. Inspired by Harrison's initial birthday fund-raiser, charity: water began encouraging others to give up presents on their birthdays and ask for contributions to help drill wells instead.[39] Participants set up a webpage announcing the venture and sent out invites to family, friends, and colleagues and also (you guessed it) to weak and dormant ties. The birthday donations have raised a lot of money for clean water but, perhaps more importantly, have also raised even more awareness. As friends told friends who told other friends, word spread quickly. It wasn't long before well-known businesspeople and celebrities were setting up pages of their own and spreading the word to their vast followings. Skateboard legend Tony Hawk raised over $20,000 for his forty-fourth birthday. Twitter founder Jack Dorsey has given up his birthday three times and raised almost $200,000.[40]

The birthday pledges also morphed as word of charity: water spread. As fund-raisers reached out to their weak ties, these people learned about charity: water and developed their own unique ideas. One person climbed a mountain to raise money; another swam the English Channel.[41] Donors saw every detail of these ventures—the total amount raised and later the project that was funded, along with photos and GPS coordinates. The innovation and transparency that charity: water had brought to the philanthropic world was immense, and it likely wouldn't have happened if Scott Harrison hadn't been forced to reach back to his former life and his dormant ties. While few folks from the nightclub world are still actively involved in charity: water (Harrison believes the tech industry is now their biggest influence and champion), the path Harrison traveled down would have looked a lot different if it weren't for those original weak ties.

The chances of unlocking value from only your immediate and close connections are minimal, since your close contacts don't have access to a lot of information you don't already have yourself. But the lessons of weak ties research, as evidenced by the experiences of White and the Fertittas, as well as Scott Harrison and charity: water, suggest that you may be missing out on a major asset: those weak ties you may have forgotten about or haven't reconnected with in a while. It's those weak ties that give you the best chance of finding new information and learning about unexpected opportunities. Moreover, weak and dormant ties are likely to be much more plentiful in your network than your strong connections. If you want to maximize the value of your network, then you need to make sure you're using *all* of your connections and not limiting yourself to just your current strong ties. The bottom line is that when it comes to new information and opportunities, your weak and dormant ties are much stronger.

FROM SCIENCE TO PRACTICE

The biggest implication of the strength of weak and dormant ties is that we ought to fight our impulses. When we have a career setback, for example, we tend to tell only a close circle of friends who may or may not be able to help (most likely not), and then we take to blindly responding to job postings online or calling headhunters. Instead, we ought to go to our weak and dormant ties, tell them our story, and see what opportunities they can steer us toward.

Even better is to start a regular practice of reengaging with your weak and dormant ties. So here's a weekly routine to get you started:

1. Like the executives studied, list six to ten work colleagues with whom you used to have a strong relationship but who have since fallen by the wayside—include, at a minimum, those colleagues with whom you haven't had an in-depth conversation in two years.
2. Randomly select one person from the list. Roll dice or flip a coin if you have to, then email or call with an invitation to chat in person or via phone call.
3. Don't set an agenda. Don't say you are looking for something specific. Just say you would like to reconnect. During a free-flowing conversation, however, you are likely to talk about work matters, problems, opportunities, etc. Make a note of these and follow up anywhere you could help or might need help.

Practicing Online

Whether you consider yourself a technology Luddite and don't have a social media profile on websites like Facebook or LinkedIn or you've grown up alongside a digital presence, you are in luck. Most of these services have an option to import your email or smartphone's address book and send invitations to connect to anyone who is a match. If you have old contacts in there, then the service will automatically do step 1 and step 2 for you. It's still on you, however, to be brave and send the invitation to chat; the technology for that isn't quite here yet.

For a downloadable template to use when completing this exercise, go to http://davidburkus.com/resources/ and look for networking resources.

— 2 —

SEE YOUR WHOLE NETWORK

Or
Why It Really Is a
Small World After All

We often think of networks as just a collection of connections we have — big or small, good or bad — and tend to sort these folks by their usefulness to the situation at hand. However, research shows that we are all so closely connected that this is a bad way to frame our networks. The truth is that we are all one big network, and the people who succeed are not the ones with the best collection but the ones who can see and navigate their network best.

In 1994, THREE POSSIBLY INEBRIATED fraternity brothers changed our understanding of human connection.

That might be a stretch, but it's not far off. The three men, Craig Fass, Brian Turtle, and Mike Ginelli, all students at Albright College in Reading, Pennsylvania, were watching movies together and started to wonder why Kevin Bacon appeared to be in so many different movies.[1] That very day, they had watched multiple movies in succession, and all of them had an appearance by Bacon. They began to speculate that perhaps Bacon was the center of the Hollywood universe. Indeed, this was the beginning of the Kevin Bacon network, or as it's known, "six degrees of Kevin Bacon." (As we'll find out, the name is derived from a well-known phenomenon called "six degrees of separation.")

To test their theory, they began to play a game. Being movie buffs, they started to name random actors and actresses and see how many steps it took to connect those people back to Kevin Bacon through movies. For example, Elvis Presley is connected to Kevin Bacon by just one intermediary. Presley was in *King Creole* with Walter Matthau, who was in *JFK* with Kevin Bacon.[2] The trio gave Presley a "Bacon number" of 2. Tom Cruise's Bacon number is 1; that's because he acted in *A Few Good Men* with Bacon. Even actors from long ago can connect to Bacon with relative ease. Marilyn Monroe has a Bacon number of just 2. (Monroe acted in *The Misfits* with Kevin McCarthy, who acted in *Hero at Large* with Kevin Bacon.)

Convinced they had stumbled upon a discovery of earth-shattering proportions, the frat brothers sent off a letter to *The Jon Stewart Show*, a late-night show on MTV popular with college students. Their letter was short but to the point: "We are three men on a mission. Our mission is to prove to the Jon Stewart audience, nay, the world, that Bacon is God."[3] Shockingly, their letter worked. They were invited to come on the show and to demonstrate their expertise by connecting Kevin Bacon to actors named at random. They also got the chance to meet Bacon himself on the show and earn their own Bacon number of sorts. Their appearance on the show made an impact and the game "Six Degrees of Kevin Bacon" spread rapidly. For their efforts, the frat brothers even landed a book deal.

More interestingly, the television show was watched by two computer science students at the University of Virginia who took the game to another level. Glen Watson and Brett Tjaden happened to be watching that fateful episode and decided that determining the number of connections between two actors might be a viable project for their studies, if only they could find the data.[4] Luckily, another computer programmer had already compiled that data a few years before when he launched the Internet Movie Database, or IMDb. That website featured information about almost every movie ever released, including everyone who worked on the film as a director, writer, producer, or actor.

It was the precise data Watson and Tjaden needed. After only a few weeks of programming and refining, they launched The Oracle of Bacon, a website where anyone can enter the names of any two movie stars and in seconds the program will find the shortest distance between them. (While the website will enter "Kevin Bacon" as a default, you can delete his name and replace it to find the connection between two non-Bacon stars.) Fueled by the popularity of the game, and offering the chance to referee debates between players, the website quickly took off. At its high point, it was receiving 20,000 visits per day. And it was also inspiring copycat games. "Six Degrees of Marlon Brando" became a fad in Germany. And in the midst of the Monica Lewinsky scandal, the *New York Times* even printed a diagram called "Six Degrees of Monica" connecting her to famous (and infamous) people like Bill Clinton (obviously), O. J. Simpson, and even Kevin Bacon. (Currently, the website is run by a different programmer, Patrick Reynolds, who rebuilt it in 1999.) In 2007, inspired by his six degrees fame, Bacon himself established a charitable organization to pair celebrities with local, less well-known charities in need of help raising awareness for their cause.[5]

While Kevin Bacon is undoubtedly the best-known person to have a numbers game revolve around him, he actually isn't the first. That title belongs to Paul Erdős, a mathematician famous for not just his productivity (more than 1,500 published papers) but his frequent collaborations (more than 500 collaborators).[6] Mathematicians today make a game of how close they are to Erdős through publications. Those original 500 collaborators have an Erdős number of 1, those with whom they collaborated have a number of 2 (unless they also collaborated directly with Erdős). The American Mathematical Society even maintains its own version of the Oracle of Bacon website for Erdős, a "collaboration distance" calculator that can link any two mathematicians.[7] The tool includes a special button that uses "Erdős" in place of a second name. Interestingly, Paul Erdős currently has a Bacon number of 3, having played himself in the documentary *N Is a Number: A Portrait of Paul Erdős* (which also featured Ronald Graham, who was in *Director's Cut* with Dave Johnson, who was in *Frost/Nixon* with Kevin Bacon).

The explanation for why such games work goes back even further than Paul Erdős and reveals something much bigger about the nature of human connection. The Bacon and Erdős numbers work because their respective industries are relatively small, but the entire world, as the social psychologist Stanley Milgram first theorized, works a bit like the Oracle of Kevin Bacon and we are all connected to each other by just a few short links.

Six Degrees of Everyone

Stanley Milgram was a professor at Harvard University with a reputation for designing genius, but controversial, experiments in human behavior and interpersonal relations. Before coming to Harvard, Milgram had conducted a study at Yale that tested the limits of individuals' willingness to obey authority, even when doing so seemed to cause harm to another human. This "obedience to authority" study became so famous that it's often referred to as the "Milgram experiment."[8] But his follow-up work may have been even more influential.

An avid traveler, Milgram would visit far-off lands like Madagascar or Pago Pago.[9] Wherever he went, he liked to play a peculiar game. He would find a complete stranger, usually someone local to the area, and introduce himself. Then he would set about trading contacts with that stranger to see if by chance they happened to have any friends in common. It was this little game that inspired Milgram and his student Jeffrey Travers to investigate just how connected we all are.

To start their experiment, Milgram and Travers first chose a target individual, a stockbroker working in Boston who was living in nearby Sharon, Massachusetts.[10] Then they picked as far off a location as they could think of. To Milgram, a New Yorker living in Boston, the choice of Omaha, Nebraska,[11] seemed most appropriate because, as he wrote, it appeared "vaguely 'out there' on the Great Plains or somewhere."[12] With the city chosen, the two psychologists went about recruiting participants.

In total, Milgram and Travers solicited 296 volunteers. From that group, around one-third were randomly chosen from the Omaha population. Another third were from Omaha, but were chosen from a list of blue-chip stockholders (who were presumably more likely to find a connection to a Boston-based stockbroker). The final third were actually from Boston (again presumably, to provide an easier route to their target individual and hence act as a sort of control group). These individuals, regardless of which of the three groups their names were drawn from, would be the starting link in a chain of connections that might lead back to the Boston stockbroker.

Every participant then received an official-looking booklet in the mail, emblazoned with the Harvard University logo.[13] This "passport"—as the experimenters called it—included instructions on how to get it to the target stockbroker as well as how to keep track of where it was sent. If participants knew the target directly, they were free to send the booklet to him. If they didn't, then they were instructed to send it to someone they knew on a first-name basis who would stand a better chance of getting the booklet to the target. They could send it to a friend living in Massachusetts, or to a local contact working in finance, or to anyone else they decided would be the best person to help the passport find its home. Included in each packet was a set of "tracer" cards, small preaddressed postcards to be sent back to Travers and Milgram so that they could also keep track of which participants had forwarded the passports.

Within only a few days, passports started arriving at the stockbroker's office.[14] The first had made it to Boston with only two intermediate connections. In total, of the 296 passports sent out, 64 of them reached their target.[15] Among all 64 passports that arrived, the average chain of connections was 5.2 people in length. Even for the Nebraska groups, the mean length was 5.5. (These are the averages of all passports that reached the target, hence the decimals. It's probably better to think of it as five to six people in length.) There was no significant difference between being actively invested in stocks and being chosen at random. Rounding up to avoid having half of a person, that is six people—six degrees of separation between randomly chosen people and a specified target living halfway across the country. Surprisingly, the small group of Boston-based participants fared only slightly better. While statistically significant, their chains were still 4.4 connections in length (or four to five people). One possible explanation is that a large portion of the passports that arrived were first sent to someone geographically much closer to the stockbroker, and from there the length of the chain was basically the same as those that had originated in Boston.

While the first step in this experiment was certainly interesting, the penultimate one was even more so. Of the 64 letters that the stockbroker received, almost half were delivered by the same three people. In fact, 25 percent of them were delivered by just one person.

Word of Travers and Milgram's experiment spread quickly. In addition to publishing their findings in a peer-reviewed journal, Milgram also wrote about the experiment in the popular press magazine *Psychology Today*.[16] To Milgram, the experiment explained why he was so often able to find a connection to complete strangers in even the most distant foreign lands he visited. His result suggested that we are all connected to each other, amazingly, by just a few introductions. But as stunning as these findings were, Travers and Milgram's experiment could only reveal the short path. It couldn't truly explain how these networks worked. However, three decades later, two scientists working at Cornell University would propose a model that could explain it all.

In the late 1990s, Cornell University professor Steven Strogatz and doctoral student Duncan Watts were studying fireflies.[17] Specifically, they were studying a unique breed of firefly in Papua New Guinea that could mysteriously sync its flashing with the flashing of the flies around it. From dusk to midnight, they would somehow fall in line with the flies around them until an entire light posse (the spectacularly accurate term for a group of fireflies) would flash in unison. Observers would note whole trees of flies flashing in unison. Watts and Strogatz wanted to know why. Inside the lab, however, they were stuck.

One day, while pondering fireflies, Watts remembered something his father had once told him—that he and every other person was only six handshakes away from the president of the United States. While Milgram's research had been published,

Watts hadn't yet encountered it, so the idea seemed a little far-fetched to him. But since it was no more difficult to believe than a tree's worth of fireflies flashing in unison, he decided to look into it. He went to the library and found Milgram's paper and also Granovetter's work on the strength of weak ties. But that was about it. All of the other research he found was disappointing, and none of it offered any explanation. Wondering if maybe it could help with the firefly problem, Watts suggested that Strogatz join him in figuring out what was going on behind the scenes to explain our six degrees of separation from each other.

Both researchers saw the dilemma as inherently a math problem, one that bore a striking similarity to graph theory (a subdomain of mathematics), but few mathematicians had even bothered to touch the problem. Watts and Strogatz decided to use graphs, diagrams, and math to solve it. To begin, they drew a perfectly ordered network—a series of dots along a circle where each dot was connected only to its closest neighbors.[18] Sending a message or introducing two dots to each other would take a long time if conducted by going through each dot to arrive at the intended receiver. But when Watts and Strogatz started adding a few links across the circle randomly, something astounding happened. The communication chain shrunk exponentially even after just a few new connections were made. Using computer simulations, they started repeating the process for hundreds of new models. Each time they would start with an orderly network of a specific size and uniform connections, then add a few random connections that spanned the network and watch as the communication chain shrunk dramatically.

It only took a few links—a few people to get the letter from Omaha to Boston—to make a large and tightly clustered world suddenly very small. Watts and Strogatz had found out the reason for the small-world effect. They had found a way for social networks to feel incredibly vast and at the same time small and interconnected.

To understand how the small-world effect works, imagine you are sitting in a circle of twenty-four people and each person can speak only to the person on either side of them. Getting a message to a person across the circle from you would require going through twelve people. But now imagine that four people in the circle—not everyone, just those four—are also able to send a message across the circle. No matter where you are sitting in the circle, the number of people needed to send a message suddenly drops by around half. Those four people's ability to provide a shortcut is all it takes. Now imagine a circle of 7 billion people, with millions of them providing shortcuts for others. You would have a world connected by only a handful of introductions. In other words, you would have our world.

Watts and Strogatz quickly wrote up their findings and sent their paper off to the prestigious journal *Nature,* but not before they decided to test their hypothesis using one of the most famous small-world examples of all: Kevin Bacon. Watts and Strogatz reached out to Brett Tjaden, one of the creators of the Oracle of Bacon, and asked to borrow his data. Using his work, as well as the collection of data from IMDb, Watts and Strogatz re-created a network of films, using costarring roles as connection points. Out of roughly 225,000 actors and actresses, the path between any two individuals turned out to be shockingly small. Everyone could be connected to everyone else in less than four steps because, just as in their mathematical models, Hollywood is a tightly clustered network that includes individuals who span vast distances and provide shortcuts for everyone else.

Interestingly, however, Kevin Bacon is not one of them. While his path to everyone else is a little shorter—less than three steps—it is by no means the shortest. That honor fell to Rod Steiger, who wasn't exactly a movie star but still managed to act in 148 films across a diverse array of genres.[19] As for Bacon, he ranked 669th on the list of best-connected actors—not exactly the center of the universe.[20] While that is bad news for Bacon, it's good news for us. His rise to fame as an uber-connected actor appears to have been a historical fluke. (Had the Albright College students been watching a different television channel, it could just as easily have been "Six Degrees of Chuck Norris.") However, his short distance to others but low ranking on the list of the best-connected suggests that perhaps all of us are indeed more connected than we think. Duncan Watts wanted to know about that too.

Having codiscovered an explanation for why the small-world effect exists, Watts turned his attention to verifying it on a larger scale. Watts, along with Peter Dodds and Roby Muhamad, recreated Milgram's experiment, but used modern technology and a much bigger sample.[21] They set up a website to recruit participants, who were then randomly directed to one of eighteen target receivers across the globe. The targets ranged from university professors in the United States to policemen in Australia to technology consultants in India.

Participants were instructed to use email to relay a message by forwarding the message to a social acquaintance who could then move it closer to the target. More than 20,000 people signed up to participate, and when the experiment ended, more than 60,000 people in 166 countries had helped relay a message. In the end, the results were shockingly similar to Milgram's. Despite the vast differences in geography and the diversity of the targets, the estimated length of communication chains was between five and seven people. Unlike Milgram's study, however, there was no common path traveled. Instead of two to three people who dominated the final leg of delivery, messages reached the end target through about as many participants as there were communication chains. "Ordinary individuals," Watts later wrote, "are just as capable of spanning critical divides between social and professional circles, between different nations, or between different neighborhoods, as exceptional people."[22]

Kevin Bacon isn't the center of the universe. No one is.

And that universe might be even smaller than we first anticipated. Since 2011, Facebook has been partnering with mathematicians and sociologists to track the degrees of separation between its users.[23] Intriguingly, as the number of users increases and the span of the globe with access to Facebook widens, the distance between users continues to shrink. In 2011, 721 million people had Facebook accounts, and the chain length between users was 3.74 people (three to four people). When Facebook ran the study again in 2016, the number of users had more than doubled, to 1.59 billion, and yet the chain length had shrunk, to 3.57 (still three to four people, but incrementally much closer to just three). In other words, if you have a Facebook account, you are within four introductions of anyone else in the billion-plus network.

It's important to note one small caveat, however. Facebook calculated the degrees of separation for people based on what was possible and found that 3.57 was the average. By contrast, both Milgram in his original study and Watts and his research teams asked participants to take action and then they traced those actions. Nevertheless, Facebook's findings suggest that of the more than 7 billion people on the planet, the possibility for connection is much less than what Watts and Milgram found. We might actually be within far fewer than six degrees of separation from anyone else. We might be far more connected than any of us would suspect.

Perhaps Milgram knew that. While we tend to refer to Travers and Milgram's study as evidence of "six degrees of separation," Milgram himself never used the term.[24] That term originated from John Guare, who wrote a play in 1990 inspired by the findings of network science. The play, and the movie that followed it, features a monologue toward the end from one of the main characters:

> I read somewhere that everybody on this planet is separated by only six other people. Six degrees of separation. Between us and everybody else on this planet. The president of the United States. A gondolier in Venice. Fill in the names . . . It's not just big names. It's anyone. A native in a rain forest. A Tierra del Fuegan. An Eskimo. I am bound to everyone on this planet by a trail of six people. It's a profound thought . . . How every person is a new door, opening up into other worlds.[25]

Guare's play outlines the real lesson of research into small worlds and the research on degrees of separation: *We don't grow or create a network—the truth is, we already exist inside of one.* Our network is not a Rolodex separate from us, to be used by us. Rather, we are an integrated part of the bigger whole. The entire collection of humans, 7 billion strong and counting, is basically one interconnected network. Everyone is a friend of a friend (even if we haven't met that friend yet). Every new person we meet opens up our ability to navigate that network, and any given person can open us up to an entirely new world.

Navigating the Network

It was knowing how to navigate that new network that landed Michelle McKenna-Doyle her dream job with the National Football League. Growing up, McKenna-Doyle was always a fan of sports. School sports were dominantly male then, but that didn't stop her from trying out for just about every team—including football. "I didn't make it obviously," McKenna-Doyle joked.[26] But she did take just about every job at her high school that got her close to the action. From painting lines on the football field to selling hot dogs at the concession stand, she did whatever she could to stay close to the game.

Her passion for football ran in the family. Her father was a devoted fan of legendary quarterback Joe Namath, and her brother accepted a full scholarship to play football at the University of Alabama. Indeed, her father was almost certain he would see his child make it to the NFL one day. And he was right—it just wasn't his son. McKenna-Doyle decided to study accounting and chose to go to Auburn University (a decision that didn't go over so well in her Crimson Tide family). There she continued operating around football, working in the Auburn Athletics Department, where she once tutored football great Bo Jackson. After graduation, McKenna-Doyle pretty much tucked away her dream of working in and around football. Instead, she worked in accounting and finance for a number of years before finding her way to the Walt Disney Company, where her fourteen years of service transitioned her from a strictly finance role to an IT role collecting and analyzing massive amounts of customer data to improve the guest experience. Eventually she became chief information officer (CIO) at Universal Orlando Resort.

McKenna-Doyle continued pivoting and moving, eventually becoming the CIO at Constellation Energy, which at the time was a Fortune 500 energy company based in Baltimore. When Exelon announced in 2011 that it was purchasing Constellation and moving the corporate headquarters to Chicago, McKenna-Doyle was faced with one more big move—either packing up and moving her home to Chicago or moving to a new job. "I didn't want to move to Chicago," McKenna-Doyle reflected. "So it was sort of in my mind that I needed to look but I didn't want to look for another job."[27] That's when her love of football guided her career once again.

While online to manage her fantasy football team, McKenna found herself wandering around on the NFL website. "There was a link down at the bottom, 'About Us,' and there was one for jobs."[28] McKenna-Doyle started reading the job openings listed and found one that sounded familiar. It wasn't listed as a CIO position, but the requirements matched her experience almost perfectly. "I read the description and I was like, 'They need a CIO.'" When she showed the job posting to her husband, he confirmed her suspicion—he said it sounded just like her. At the time, she didn't know anyone working at the NFL or have any way to break through the clutter of blind job applications, so she put the thought of working there in the back of her mind.

A few days later, a friend forced it back to the front of her mind. The friend had found the same job posting online, and she sent it to McKenna-Doyle along with a note saying how much it sounded like her. "Alright, that's two people," McKenna-Doyle thought, and with that confirmation she resolved to apply.[29] The only problem was that she didn't have any connection straight to the executive offices of the NFL. Moreover, she would have to convince the leadership of the league that what the NFL actually needed wasn't the job they'd posted, but rather a full-scale CIO with a seat at the senior leadership table. Pulling that off from just a random online application would be nearly impossible, so she knew she needed to get closer to those making the hiring decision. She just didn't know how . . . at first.

Even among her weak ties, there just wasn't anyone who was working for the league. But a few degrees out, there was a path that could get her there.

"I started working my network," McKenna-Doyle said, "and someone I used to work with at Disney was at Russell Reynolds."[30] This person was a former Disney cast member who had gone on to become a headhunter at the well-known executive search firm. Neither he nor his firm was conducting the search, but he happened to know the firm that was, and how to get their attention. He connected McKenna-Doyle to the right search firm, which then, in turn, connected her to the NFL. With the connection made, she was able to sell herself and her idea to the leadership team. It took some time, but after six months going back and forth, the NFL had made McKenna-Doyle an offer—to become Senior Vice President and CIO.

When she started with the NFL, McKenna-Doyle had been appointed to the highest office a female executive had ever held in the male-dominated league. And best of all, McKenna-Doyle's father finally got to see one of his children make it to the NFL. McKenna-Doyle's story is inspirational, offering hope that almost anyone can find meaningful work connected to their passion. But it's also a story that highlights the importance of six degrees of separation and the realization that we are all operating inside of a larger network. The network of friends of friends can be a powerful tool even when we don't know someone directly. The lesson of the small-world effect, and the lesson of six degrees of separation is that certain people aren't the center of the universe—all of us are. And all of us can find a path through the network to reach the stars.

FROM SCIENCE TO PRACTICE

As we learned in the first chapter, there's an incredible power lying dormant in your dormant ties. Old contacts with whom you have fallen out of touch often have access to new information. However, as we saw in this chapter, former contacts are even more valuable than that. The most common reason for a formerly strong tie turning dormant is that either you or that person has moved on. One of you may have physically moved to a different location, or switched jobs, or just moved on to a different stage in life.

But when you move, you don't just leave—you also arrive somewhere new. As Michelle McKenna-Doyle found out when she started navigating her network, often when someone moves they become a valuable connection to new parts of the larger network. Connecting with old contacts gives you a larger sense of your network and just how many potential connections are within your reach. In other words, former colleagues are more valuable than you might think.

One of the best ways to stay connected to, or get back in touch with, these former colleagues is through alumni networks. While McKenna-Doyle didn't have a formal alumni group to use, she did a great job keeping in touch with her former Disney colleagues, and it paid off.

Today it's even easier. Most universities maintain a fairly active alumni network (they see it as a source of future donations), and many companies and even nonprofit organizations are starting to organize alumni networks to keep connected to former members (they see them as a valuable source of information, just as the research on dormant ties would predict). In addition, trade associations and professional groups are a great place not just to expand your network with new connections but to reconnect with former contacts who have moved into new roles but stayed in the same profession.

If you can't find any alumni network, trade association, or professional group through which to reconnect, then why not start your own? It doesn't have to be elaborate. Simply reaching out to former coworkers and inviting them to have lunch or call just to catch up may be enough to kick-start an alumni movement. Interestingly, this is exactly what happened at Procter & Gamble. Former employees started a nonprofit alumni club that grew to be so influential that P&G chose to deliberately partner with them to serve all former P&G employees and their community. Now the P&G alumni network rivals that of more deliberate efforts like those of universities and consulting firms.

Practicing Online

Social media services like Facebook and LinkedIn are a great place to reconnect with old colleagues and start getting a feel for the larger network you have access to within a few introductions. Both of these services (and other social media websites) offer a "Groups" function that enables any individual to establish a group around interests, location, or former employees. Even if your former organizations don't have formal alumni networks, the chances are pretty good that someone has created an online rendition. And if not, these services lower the cost of starting your own to nothing.

For a downloadable template to use when completing this exercise, go to http://davidburkus.com/resources/ and look for networking resources.

— 3 —

BECOME A BROKER AND FILL STRUCTURAL HOLES

Or
Why Climbing the Corporate Ladder May Be the Worst Path to the Top

We often think that the way to success is to just stay in our lane, climb up the corporate ladder or become an expert in our field, and focus on meeting ever more powerful people inside our industry or sector. Research into networks reveals that, surprisingly, the most connected people inside a tight group within a single industry are less valuable than the people who span the gaps between groups and broker information back and forth. This finding has implications for how we manage our careers and how we manage our organizations.

JANE McGONIGAL HAD TO CHOOSE between playing video games and healing from head trauma. She chose both, and it saved her life.

In the summer of 2009, McGonigal was in her office and reached down to pick up some papers. On the way back up, she hit her head hard on the cabinet door. Nothing major, she thought, but she knew something wasn't right. "That wasn't good at all," she told her husband after it happened.[1] A few hours later, she started to feel weird. Within a day, she was experiencing headaches, vertigo, and slurred speech. She found that she couldn't read or write without triggering symptoms. Something seemed like it was indeed major after all.

McGonigal went to see the doctor, who diagnosed her with a concussion and sent her home, saying she would feel better after a week's rest. After a week, though, she wasn't any better. A week turned into a month of symptoms, and doctors changed their recovery estimate to three months. She wasn't healing properly from the concussion, they said, and so the symptoms would last much longer. Her doctors told her to avoid everything that would trigger symptoms. No reading or writing. No exercise. No work. No alcohol or caffeine. No video games. "In other words," she joked to her doctor, "no reason to live."[2]

It turned out that she wouldn't have to wait through three months of doing nothing. Thirty-four days after getting hit on the head, she had her "aha" moment—but it wasn't what most people would expect.

I'm either going to kill myself or turn this into a game, she thought.[3]

Her suicidal thought wasn't that uncommon. One in three people with a traumatic brain injury, even a mild one, start to fall into a depression and can so strongly doubt they will recover that they ponder ending their lives. In the moment, McGonigal's mind was telling her that she would never get better and that she wanted to die.

Her idea to turn the experience into a game, however, was not so common. In fact, it was an idea that might have occurred only to her.

For almost a decade before her accident, McGonigal had been studying the psychology of games and designing video games that make the world a better place.[4] When she started her career,

McGonigal was working as a game designer in New York City on various commercial projects, but that life wasn't fully living up to her expectations. She had a twin sister who had moved to California to study psychology at Stanford and who helped convince her to move out west. McGonigal enrolled at the University of California at Berkeley in a PhD program in performance studies. The degree plan was flexible enough that she could mold it to her interests, which involved a blend of psychology and her game design background.

Armed with this new knowledge, and at the intersection of games and social science, McGonigal started working on projects that leveraged the passion and creativity of gaming with social problems.[5] She created a six-week simulation called "World Without Oil" in which players have to find ways to outlast a fictional oil shortage. Then she worked with the World Bank to create "Evoke," a game in which players have to develop ways to help eliminate poverty. "Evoke" would give birth to about fifty businesses and social organizations that would put the players' ideas into practice in the real world. Throughout all her work, McGonigal laid out her case that games aren't just an escape from life, but that they can truly improve human lives.

Now, sitting in bed with a brain injury, McGonigal was challenged more than ever to prove her thesis. Could she design a game that would help her heal?

She called her game "Jane the Concussion Slayer," a nod to her favorite fictional heroine, Buffy the Vampire Slayer.[6] She recruited allies like her sister and her husband to help her, and together they established challenges she could take on that would help her healing process and also help her avoid the "bad guys" that triggered her symptoms. At the end of each day, they tallied up a score of how well she did.

In a surprisingly short period of time, the game had helped her get better. Many of her physical symptoms remained, but her mental symptoms started to dissipate. Her feelings of depression and anxiety lifted, and over time she started to both look and feel stronger. "Even when I still had the symptoms, even while I was in pain, *I stopped suffering*," she said. "I felt more in control of my own destiny."[7]

After a few months of playing the game, McGonigal went public. She posted her experience online, along with a brief video explaining how to play. And she changed the game's name. During her recovery, so many people had told her to "get better soon," and in a brave response to them, she decided she didn't just want to be better—she wanted to be "SuperBetter," and thus the new name of the game was born.

Soon, McGonigal was hearing from people all over the world who were playing their own version of "SuperBetter." They were using the game not only to help battle chronic pain and depression but also to recover from the stress of losing a job or going through a painful romantic breakup. More than half a million people have now played "SuperBetter" as a way to get exactly that—super better. The game has also helped McGonigal with more than just the original concussion incident. When she and her husband were trying to have children, she played a version of the game again. And when those children, twins, were born ten weeks early, she and her husband used the game to get through two harrowing months in the NICU.[8]

But McGonigal wasn't satisfied with just lots of "SuperBetter" players and great case studies. She wanted to study "SuperBetter" itself to either prove that the game could be useful in the recovery process or modify it in order to make it so. She wanted to connect the worlds of video games and medicine to create games that could heal. Her mission took her to the University of Pennsylvania and the renowned scientist Dr. Martin Seligman. Seligman is the father of positive psychology, the study of achievement, flourishing, and life satisfaction (as opposed to much of psychology's focus on mental illness). At the time, Seligman was studying the essential elements of a meaningful life, and McGonigal was studying his research. When they finally met, she got right to the point and explained how "SuperBetter" could help. She felt that what she was doing with "SuperBetter" and what Seligman had discovered with his research on what makes for a meaningful life were going in the same direction. "It's a perfect match," she told him.[9]

Seligman didn't push back; instead, he leaned in. He thought McGonigal's research was indeed interesting and invited her to work alongside him. Soon they were collaborating with fellow Penn researcher Ann Marie Roepke on a randomized, controlled study of the "SuperBetter" method as a treatment for depression and anxiety. They found that playing the game helped to significantly reduce symptoms and increase happiness and satisfaction. That led McGonigal to work on a clinical trial at Ohio State University, with funding from the National Institutes of Health (NIH). Her study found that "SuperBetter" improved mood and decreased suffering and anxiety during rehabilitation.

McGonigal isn't done yet. Beyond designing games, she views her role as a liaison between the gamer community and the world of scientific and medical research—a gap that she feels desperately needs to be spanned. And as we'll soon discover, the secret to a lot of professional success and meaningful impact lies in spanning gaps.

"There are more than 1,000 studies that have done a really good job of trying to figure out what are the features of different games that produce different benefits, but they're all behind academic firewalls," she explained. "We have 1.23 billion people on the planet who spend, on average, an hour a day playing video games. What percentage of them can access the papers?"[10] Fewer than 1 percent, by her estimate.

"I'm really trying to help make sure people have access to the really practical findings that can help them lead happier, healthier lives," she said further. "SuperBetter" is just one tool in that effort. McGonigal sees how much more work she has to do. One of her more jovial goals, she jokes, is to see a game designer win the Nobel Prize for Medicine—though not her and not "SuperBetter." (McGonigal says she would give it to the inventor of Tetris.) While she may not get a Nobel medallion anytime soon, McGonigal can be sure that she has helped almost as many lives as some of the Nobel winners of the past. Indeed, around 1 million people have now used "SuperBetter" to become super better.[11] In addition, her work alongside medical and scientific researchers will help millions more.

While the origins of Jane McGonigal's story are unique, and her game is certainly an original creation, the explanation for the great impact of her work is not unique at all. She took advantage of a type of opportunity that is actually fairly common in networks: because her work spans a structural hole in the bigger social network that she operates inside of, she creates tremendous value for others. From the moment she left New York City to study at Berkeley, she was on a path that would blend insights from both social science and video game design and force the two communities to talk to one other. She generated enormous value for both communities by being that liaison. And by learning how she and others did it, you can too.

Going for Broker

As individuals tend to operate mostly inside of tight-knit communities or clusters, often spaces form between those clusters. Ronald Burt, a sociologist now at the University of Chicago, first theorized about the opportunities inside these gaps in the social structure, or, as he labeled them, "structural holes." At first Burt didn't refer to groups of contacts who all know each other as clusters. He chose to call them, perhaps more appropriately, a redundancy. When everyone knows everyone else in the local cluster, the contacts are redundant—individual contacts don't provide any added benefit from others in the cluster. "People who spend a lot of time with the same other people often get to know one another," Burt wrote.[12] And when everyone in the local cluster knows or has access to the same information as everyone else, the contacts are likewise redundant. Inside of these clusters, as we have seen, information can move fast and collaboration happens easily, but the downside is that information tends to stay stuck inside the cluster and new information from outside rarely enters.

In contrast, "a structural hole," Burt wrote, "is a relationship of non-redundancy between two contacts. The hole is a buffer, like an insulator in an electric circuit."[13] This isn't to say that those inside of clusters—those redundant connections—are typically unaware of other people. (Although as we'll see in a future chapter, they can easily become oblivious to anyone outside the cluster.) More likely, they are aware of other groups but lack a connection to them. They are focused on the activities inside of their group and don't attend to the need to bridge the gap between their group and others. As such, they lack both a way to gain new information and a way to share their information with others. Burt asserted, rather logically, that the gaps between clusters come with a large information advantage, and that those who span the gap are able to leverage that advantage. Indeed, the people who fill structural holes—the *brokers,* as they would later be labeled—end up with control over the flow of information and eventually with more power than those who just sit inside of a cluster. "People whose networks span structural holes have early access to diverse, often contradictory, information and interpretations, which gives them a competitive advantage in seeing good ideas," Burt wrote.[14]

This is exactly what happened over 200 years ago when a Native American named Sequoyah single-handedly brought language to the Cherokee Nation. Sequoyah was trained as a silversmith, a job that brought him into frequent contact with American settlers.[15] He learned English and eventually learned to write his name as a signature on his silver work. He also served as a soldier in the US Army during the Creek War of 1813–1814. He didn't serve long, but long enough to watch how letters sent to and from the battle lines were keeping soldiers in touch with their commanders, and of course with their loved ones. Sequoyah committed to bringing the gift of written communication to his own people, who at the time were so far removed from the concept that they attributed writing to a form of sorcery. It took him years of trial and error, and lots of borrowing of symbols from Greek, Roman, Cyrillic, and Arabic characters, but he eventually created an alphabet of symbols for each of the eighty-six syllables in the Cherokee language.

When he presented his alphabet to the Cherokee Nation, they were initially skeptical and, by some reports, put Sequoyah on trial for witchcraft. But during the trial he demonstrated how easy it was to learn his system. Within weeks, thousands of Cherokee had adopted the alphabet. Sequoyah's alphabet allowed for the creation of *The Cherokee Phoenix,* the first Native American newspaper—itself sort of a broker between two clusters, as it was published in both Cherokee and English. Sam Houston, the prominent Texas politician, reportedly said to Sequoyah, "Your invention of the alphabet is worth more to your people than two bags full of gold in the hands of every Cherokee."[16] The alphabet remains in use today and can be seen all over Tahlequah, Oklahoma, the capital of Cherokee Nation—where the alphabet is still used on street signs (alongside English) and taught in public schools. Sequoyah's invention is one of only a few times in human history that a lone individual of a preliterate society developed an original writing system. And it never would have happened had Sequoyah not been a broker between the early American community and the Cherokee Nation.

In the modern day, studies show, the brokers who span structural holes between clusters, even if they don't invent new languages or create games that heal, go on to more productive and rewarding careers. In one study, Ronald Burt demonstrated that brokers between groups are often paid more, are promoted more often, and have the best chance of coming up with innovative new ideas. Burt surveyed 673 managers at a large electronics company who ran the supply chain for the entire firm. All managers were asked for an idea to improve the supply chain operation: "From your perspective, what is the one thing that you would change to improve [the company's] supply chain management?"[17] This simple question yielded 455 ideas. Managers were also asked if they had discussed their idea with anyone. Then they were asked to identify the persons with whom they generally discussed supply chain issues. They were also asked to describe how long they had known each of these contacts and how strong their connection to each one was. From the responses, Burt was able to draw a rough map of the informal network, outlining who talked with whom and who had more diverse connections than average.

From there, Burt deferred to the judgment of top management. He asked two senior managers at the firm, both with significant experience in running a supply chain, to evaluate each idea based on how much value would be generated if it were implemented. Because he was working closely with the company, Burt also secured data on salaries, performance evaluations, promotions, and time in rank for each manager. When he took all this data and compared it to the network map, he saw that *brokers—those who were discussing ideas with individuals from other clusters or groups of the organization—were significantly more likely to have valuable ideas for improvement*. Or, as he wrote, "People who stand near the holes in a social structure are at higher risk of having good ideas."[18] Moreover, the brokers inside the firm's network were more likely to be paid highly, to receive positive performance evaluations, and to be promoted. Clearly, those individuals who have both access to diverse information and the ability to combine that information to create new ideas provide value not just to the company but to themselves.

Burt's theory of structural holes has been validated time and again by other researchers from a variety of fields. But all of this research begs one important question: how do you build a career as a broker? Two decades after Burt first proposed his theory of structural holes, the researcher Adam Kleinbaum may have found an answer. Kleinbaum, a professor at Tuck School of Business at Dartmouth College, conducted a study inside a large information technology firm.[19] Like Burt, Kleinbaum first began by recruiting employees and surveying their contacts. Unlike Burt, however, Kleinbaum didn't just ask them to list a few contacts. Even better, he got access to employees' emails.

For several decades, network research relied on written

surveys that asked subjects to list their acquaintances and report what type of relationship they had with each one. Indeed, this is how Burt's own studies were often conducted. But this method got a strong upgrade when email became commonplace in organizations. Instead of relying on subjects' memory, now researchers like Kleinbaum had access to high-quality data that tracked communication among the various contacts in almost real time.

Kleinbaum collected three months' worth of email communication from these volunteer employees, representing an astounding 30,262 people inside the firm. (While he didn't reveal the name of the firm, the sheer size of the network explains why he chose the pseudonym "BigCo.") Kleinbaum removed all the mass communications and blind carbon copies to focus on just the deliberate messages sent by and received from employees. From that data, he was able to construct a rough network map of the organization.

Kleinbaum also collected human resource data from each of the volunteer employees in the sample. This included employees' demographic data, like gender, but also their salary level and career path over a period of seventy-seven months, including their business unit, job function, and location. When he finally looked at the complete picture, Kleinbaum found something surprising. The individuals most likely to become brokers and to develop connections across structural holes were what he called "organizational misfits." Instead of pursuing the slow and steady ladder-climbing career paths of most employees, these misfits had atypical career paths, bouncing around to different business units and filling different job functions. "The more diverse an actor's career history across groups, the more likely that actor is to engage in improbable category-spanning communication," he wrote.[20]

The findings make sense intuitively. That is, if your career path takes you to various clusters inside an organization and you keep your relationships active, you are much more likely to have a diverse set of relationships than if you merely climb upward inside the same leg of the organizational chart. However, the findings run counter to much of our conventional wisdom about how to grow a career inside of a company or industry. We are told, and often tell others, to work hard, keep your head down, and just focus on climbing the ladder. But taken together, the research on structural holes suggests that jumping from ladder to ladder is a more effective strategy, and that lateral or even downward moves across an organization are more promising in the longer run because that is how new and diverse contacts are developed. In contrast, the traditional advice might actually bring diminishing returns as more and more new contacts turn out to be redundant.

In addition to employees' individual careers, organizations that push an "up or out" development path of climbing up the career ladder might be unknowingly causing harm to themselves. Focusing everyone on steady forward progress does little to create the structural holes that an organization needs to innovate and survive. And sometimes, when survival is threatened, taking steps to build and create new brokers for structural holes is the only tactic that can save an organization. That is what General Stanley McChrystal discovered when he found himself in Baghdad and in command of an operation with wide and deep structural holes and almost no way to fill them.

Filling Structural Holes

In 2003, General Stanley McChrystal took command of the US Joint Special Operations Task Force and quickly realized just how much the traditional tactics of warfare were failing in Iraq

—and just how much the structure of the military was to blame. Leading an interservice team that included the Army Rangers, the Air Force's Delta Force, and the Navy SEALs, McChrystal saw that the structure of the American armed forces left a lot of structural holes between the different branches. "Meaningful relationships between teams were nonexistent," McChrystal reflected.[21] Each team excelled at what they were trained for, but a hard-fought contest against Al Qaeda in Iraq (AQI) was not exactly what they had trained for. AQI was a fluid, ever-changing network of operatives, and the breakdowns in communication among the US military branches gave it huge opportunities. AQI thus exploited the structural holes in the armed forces, surviving and thriving against a much better resourced and trained opponent because of the gaps between each team. "To each unit, the piece of the war that really mattered was the piece inside their box on the org chart," McChrystal wrote. "They were fighting their own fights in their own silos."[22]

One of the starkest examples of this division came shortly after he took command of the Task Force. McChrystal was inspecting an intelligence facility located on a base at Baghdad International Airport when he opened the door to a supply closet and found a massive pile of burlap sacks and plastic bags. As he started to ask questions, he learned that the bags in the pile were full of evidence that had been collected by Special Forces and SEAL teams during missions and sent back to base. The teams had hastily put any evidence they discovered into whatever bags they could find, with only small tags or sometimes even just Post-It notes for explanation, before tossing the bags onto whatever transportation was headed back to base. Hours later, the evidence bags would arrive—often with the explanatory notes having fallen off—and intelligence teams would have to decipher not just the evidence but the context for why it was even being sent to them. "The operators [mission teams], adept at their own roles but having little understanding of the nuts and bolts of intel analysis, could not anticipate what sorts of explanations would be meaningful, what sort of context was relevant, or which material had to be turned around instantly and which could wait," McChrystal explained. The physical and relational distance between these two clusters led to much being lost in translation. "They did not know the analysts personally and saw them as removed and territorial," McChrystal wrote.[23] Because of that, much of the evidence had been left to gather dust in that supply closet.

McChrystal knew immediately that he had work to do. "The unopened bags of evidence were symptomatic of a larger problem," he wrote.[24] When he looked out over the organization he now led, he saw lots of teams operating brilliantly, but they worked independently in an interdependent environment against an interdependent foe. That very evening, McChrystal and his team drew out the organizational chart as it really operated and sought to identify the structural holes that were causing issues. They referred to these holes as "blinks," and they saw them everywhere. Teams in the Task Force had barely any kind of horizontal relationships. Even when stationed on the same base, teams mostly stayed within their own branch, living and working in different areas and even using different gyms. "The blinks were even worse between the Task Force and our partner organizations," McChrystal noted.[25] While the Task Force relied on intelligence from the Central Intelligence Agency, the National Security Agency, and the Federal Bureau of Investigation, its relationships with these agencies were weak. Likewise, there were large gaps between the Task Force and the other military units with which it had to cooperate.

"We needed the SEALs to trust Army Special Forces, and for them to trust the CIA," McChrystal wrote. "We didn't need every member of the Task Force to know everyone else; we just needed everyone to know *someone* on every team."[26] In other words, McChrystal needed to find a way to span the structural holes in the entire US military, or at least among the military members who were a part of his mission. He didn't need to make the entire Task Force one giant network cluster, but he did need to find a way to build a relationship between at least one person on each team or cluster and someone else on every other team —and he needed to do this for each and every team he relied on to win. In McChrystal's words, "We needed to create a team of teams."[27] In Ronald Burt's words, the Task Force needed to first create *brokers*.

One of the first ways McChrystal did that was by revamping and reenergizing the brokers who were already supposed to be present. Each military unit and intelligence agency had a role called the liaison officer. On paper, the liaison officers were supposed to be the brokers who connected the different clusters. In practice, however, these roles were usually filled by people who weren't fitting in with their previous team or who were doing one last tour before their retirement. In other words, the liaison officer position was seen as simply a sort of holding pattern for officers who were on their way out or who needed to be kept away from the action—similar to what Adam Kleinbaum would call an organizational misfit. Few people saw the liaison officer role as an enviable position. As a result, trust wasn't high and the sharing of information was poor. In many cases, liaison officers were seen by their hosts as scribes, there just to sit in on meetings, transcribe notes, and report back. In some cases, they were even considered spies. The bottom line was that nobody really looked upon liaison officers as being important to the cause.

But McChrystal knew this role was vital to building the lines of communication he needed. So he set about changing the perception of liaison officers. To do that, he started assigning his best soldiers to liaison officer roles. He took them off the front lines, traded their uniforms for business suits, and sent them to the embassies and intelligence agencies where he needed solid relationships. In the beginning, not much changed. Most people hated the idea of taking the best and brightest out of the field, and most of the host agencies didn't change their behavior just because new bodies were present in the back of the room. But over time, the skills and attitudes of these new officers started winning agencies over.

Perhaps McChrystal's most controversial action, at least at first, was the embedding program. It worked like an exchange program for military operators. McChrystal would take someone from one team like the Navy SEALs and place him with a unit of Army Special Forces. This idea was met with a lot of resistance at first. Most objectors cited how different the units' training and operational norms were—so different that these exchanges could create real liabilities. And initially, that may have been true. But over time the exchanged soldiers learned the cultural norms and behaviors of the units they were embedded in. They built positive relationships and gained the perspective on the overall mission that could only been seen from inside that unit. When they returned to their home unit, their positive experience and new perspective would spread to the other members of the team. Likewise, the unit in which those soldiers were embedded would see them as representative of the entire unit from which they came. Over time the relationship ties between units strengthened dramatically, allowing them to operate alongside each other even more impressively. "Bonds of trust began to form," McChrystal explained. "People from different tribes began to see increasingly familiar faces. Even strangers were now, by extension, part of a familiar and trusted unit."[28]

By building and strengthening these brokers and patching up structural holes, the Task Force had the capability and flexibility it needed to outmaneuver AQI. The momentum of the mission started to change, and McChrystal's new tactics brought them dramatically closer to victory. "To defeat a network, we had become a network," McChrystal would later write. "We had become a team of teams."[29]

Like Jane McGonigal, Sequoyah, and the liaison officers of the Joint Special Operations Task Force, the brokers who span structural holes create tremendous value for themselves and for the networks they serve. This may sound like a counterintuitive strategy compared to the steady kissing up and climbing of the hierarchical ladder that many assume is required of upwardly mobile networkers. But playing in between the clusters and connecting them to each other can provide huge advantages not just for brokers but also for the organizations they work with.

FROM SCIENCE TO PRACTICE

The research on structural holes sends a clear signal: there is real value to be captured by bringing two unconnected groups together. You might not always be able to see that value right away, but as you become the broker who fills the structural holes, you will have a greater chance of finding the right opportunity. Given the importance of this role, it's vital to first know whether or not you are currently a broker in your local network or, if not, who the actual brokers are.[30] Here's a quick exercise to identify whether you're a broker filling structural holes and who the brokers in your network are:

1. On a blank sheet of paper, draw three vertical lines to create three columns.
2. In the left column, list the ten to twenty-five people who have been most influential in your career (by making you aware of job openings, providing guidance or advice, assisting on vital projects, etc.).
3. In the middle column, next to each name in the left column, list the person who introduced you to that contact—that is, the person who connected you to this influential person.
4. In the right column, list anyone to whom you have introduced the contact from the left column. If you haven't introduced them to anyone, leave it blank.

In examining these three columns, pay attention to the recurring names. If one individual's name appears several times, chances are that person is an important broker in your local network, spanning key structural holes and connecting you to people you would otherwise not know. If most of your right column is blank, then there is a good chance you are not currently operating as a broker. But fortunately for you, you now have a map of the several key connections in your life and career whom you can begin to think about serving via introductions to others.

Practicing Online

If you have concluded that you need to step up your efforts and begin to be more of a broker, there are several ways social media services can help. The most common way is by examining mutual friends. Almost all online services let you see what mutual connections you and each of your contacts share. If you are introducing two people who are already connected to each other, then you are not really filling a structural hole. But you can easily find this out by looking up the connections profile and verifying that before you seek to make an introduction.

More importantly, if you are using your social media profiles to compile your list, you will also start to notice patterns in who is *not* connected to whom. You might even stumble upon the first structural hole that needs spanning.

For a downloadable template to use when completing this exercise, go to http://davidburkus.com/resources/ and look for networking resources.

— 4 —

SEEK OUT SILOS

Or

Why You Need to Spend Time in Clusters, but Not Too Much Time

While much of modern business writing warns about the dangers of silos, the truth is more complicated. Research suggests that, indeed, becoming too siloed can be damaging to businesses and careers, but at the same time, not being siloed enough can be just as damaging to growth. The most successful individuals know that they need clusters of similar people who can help them develop and grow, but also that they can't spend all of their time inside of clusters. They oscillate between being part of a silo and reaching out into the broader network.

IN 1291, THE RESIDENTS of Venice, Italy, grew tired of their glassmakers.[1]

They didn't get bored with the product. Blown glass was a unique and beautiful product that had quickly become a lucrative source of revenue for the glassmakers and a source of pride for the city. In addition, Venice's location as a hub along several trade routes made it possible to distribute the product around the world, enhancing that revenue and the prestige it brought the city. The problem was that glassmaking was a risky endeavor. To mold and shape glass into works of art, these skilled masters needed to keep their ovens around 1,000 degrees Fahrenheit. Not usually a problem—unless your oven is housed in a wooden building, in a neighborhood built mostly from wood and located on top of a series of canals. So while the Venetians were proud of these artisans' craft, they had grown weary of this craft's unfortunate tendency to burn down parts of the city.

Eventually, in an attempt to have the best of both worlds, the city government kicked the glassmakers out. They forced them to move across the Venetian Lagoon to Murano, a series of small islands about the size of a small neighborhood. In effect, the craftsmen were forced into a small silo—a tight cluster separated by water from the rest of the city. They could still reach the rest of the community, but their geographic isolation made sure that happened far less often.

Thus far, everything we've discovered about clusters suggests that this should have been a crippling blow to Venetian glassmakers. Research on weak ties and the importance of structural holes emphasizes the importance of building bridges between communities, silos, or clusters in order to create innovative ideas and generate value. Modern literature, especially business literature, is filled with warnings to avoid the damaging effects of creating silos in business and in industry.

In April 2014, General Motors' new CEO, Mary Barra, sat in a congressional oversight committee hearing to answer questions about the recent recall of 800,000 automobiles and the much less recent discovery of the failed ignition switch that had triggered it.[2] The technical problem was that, because of a weak spring, a small amount of force applied to the key when it was in the ignition—even an accidental nudge—was enough to move the car from the "run" position to the "accessory" position, which meant that safety measures like airbags would not engage in a crash. That malfunction had cost over 100 lives, many of whom were teenagers, as the inexpensive cars that used that ignition switch were a frequent choice for a first car.[3]

"There were silos of information," said Barra in her testimony. "So people had bits and pieces and didn't come forward with the information or didn't act with a sense of urgency, and it was simply unacceptable."[4] Barra herself was not informed about the issue until January 2014, the same month she took office, but GM employees, in one capacity or another, had known about the issue for nearly ten years. That is, as early as 2002, GM engineers were aware of the ignition switch problem. But the engineers working on the ignition system weren't the same employees who were working on airbags. The ignition system people didn't know that such a shutoff would keep airbags from deploying. In their small, self-contained silo, they simply saw it as a nonsafety issue and hence not a priority to fix.

GM's error is not unique to businesses. After the terror attacks of September 11, 2001, investigators sought answers as to why the vast network of intelligence services in the United States had failed to properly assess and respond to the threat of Al Qaeda. They found that the attacks would have been preventable, but that silos among the intelligence departments had kept the threat from being detected.[5] Two years prior to the 9/11 attacks, the FBI had been monitoring two of the hijackers, Khalid al-Midhar and Nawaq Alhazmi, as part of ongoing counterterrorism investigations in California. At the same time, the CIA knew about connections between the two men and terrorist organizations.

But the CIA never shared that information with the FBI. If it had, then tracking both men in San Diego as they planned and prepared would have been the best chance to undermine their plan and prevent the attacks. But the CIA silo isn't entirely to blame. The investigators also found that the National Security Agency had intercepted communications from both men and flagged them for their extremist content. In other words, had the FBI, CIA, and NSA not been so siloed—had there been a better system to fill structural holes—it's likely that the attacks could have been prevented.

Given these examples, and what we know about the importance of structural holes, it's tempting to look back at the Venetian government's forced relocation and assume that the siloed glassmakers would suffer on Murano.

But that's not what happened.

Instead, the art of glassmaking flourished in its new home. While the glassmakers were technically competitors, their unique trade (and the tendency among their families to intermarry) led them to share information and ideas. Techniques were refined, and creativity flourished. Innovations in the craft became commonplace, and the creativity of their artwork exploded.

It was on Murano that glassmakers found a way to make optically clear glass, as well as glass with threads of gold running through it. It was on Murano that glassmakers discovered how to make chandeliers, as well as fake gemstones made from glass. Murano, and by extension Venice, quickly developed a monopoly on glassmaking as Murano glass became a status symbol throughout Europe. The glassmakers themselves were elevated to a place of high prestige and became (or saw their daughters marry) the most prominent citizens of the city. The island of Murano even became known as the Isle of Glass.

And Murano isn't unique. For every example of the damaging and isolating effects of silos there's an example of how clusters in a social network help unleash creative new ideas or make individuals and teams more efficient and productive.

In 1921, Ernest Hemingway arrived in Paris, his suitcase full of letters from his friend and fellow author Sherwood Anderson.[6] The letters weren't for Hemingway to read during his trip. Instead, they were introductory letters to prominent writers living in the city. Anderson had assured Hemingway that Paris would be a great place to refine his writing skills by joining the cluster of artists and writers who had gathered there. It was through Anderson that Hemingway met Gertrude Stein, and through Stein that Hemingway found himself interacting with writers like Ezra Pound and James Joyce and artists such as Pablo Picasso.

Stein had been hosting salons of expatriate creatives who gathered to drink, socialize, discuss their work, and often drink some more. Before Hemingway left for Paris, he had shown promise as a talented writer, but mostly wrote for magazines and newspapers. It was during the Paris years that he found the collaboration and mentorship that propelled his skills. Through this unique social cluster, he also made the connections he needed to find a publisher for his novels. Without the help of Stein's community, Hemingway's work would likely only be found in archived periodicals, and not inside of nearly every high school English classroom.

Or consider another set of famous writers separated from Stein's group by about ten years and the English Channel.[7] One of the most influential activities in the writing lives of the British authors C. S. Lewis and J. R. R. Tolkien was their participation in a cluster of writers known as "The Inklings." Besides Lewis and Tolkien, the group included writers and poets like Charles Williams and Owen Barfield. (Some of the books in Lewis's "Chronicles of Narnia" are dedicated to Barfield's children.) The meetings were fairly informal, with many members joining in only sporadically. The meetings were typically held on Thursday nights, either in Lewis's rooms at Oxford University or at a local pub called The Eagle and Child (or as locals called it, "the Bird and Baby").

The writers would discuss ideas and influences, read rough drafts of novels or poems, and share feedback with one another. The purpose wasn't to cowrite anything—almost all of their writing was still done in solitude—nor was it to show off finished works. Instead, the cluster was created for giving and receiving feedback, as well as to connect with similar people, share advice and ideas, and together make each other's work stronger. It was through this cluster that Lewis and Tolkien developed their deep friendship, which survived the group's disbanding in the late 1940s. Legend has it that it was Lewis who had to argue with Tolkien that a manuscript he kept working on and reading at meetings was finally ready for print. Without Lewis and this cluster, Tolkien might never have published *The Lord of the Rings*.

So while modern writing on business and careers tends to decry silos, the undeniable fact is that when individuals are clustered together in a work group—be it a cluster in one location, a department, or a group, like The Inklings, working on individual projects—they tend to get better at what they do and require less supervision. Silos make it easier for teammates and colleagues to hold each other accountable and to communicate quickly. In fact, for some time sociologists struggled to balance the known positive effects of clusters and silos with the demonstrably positive effects of being the broker filling a structural hole. Clusters and silos are indeed important for creativity and productivity, but when they become too siloed, they can be damaging to individuals and organizations.

So how do you determine which silos to seek out and join and which ones to ignore? The answer might be a little surprising. Research suggests that the secret isn't to ask which silos to join and which to avoid, but rather to focus on how long to interact with a silo and when to move on.

When to Cluster and When to Spread

From a network science perspective, the most interesting thing about clusters is that they really shouldn't exist. That might be a little bit of overstatement, but ever since sociologists began applying the tools of mathematics and statistics to the study of human networks, they have consistently found that social networks—networks of people as opposed to, say, electrical circuits or mathematical models of nodes and lines—display higher levels of transitivity.[8] *Transitivity* is a fancy word for the idea that if person A knows person B, and B knows person C, then there's a really good chance that A and C know each other as well. Transitivity leads to clustering, the grouping together of people around each other. And while some transitivity and clustering occurs in network models drawn randomly, social networks seem to have a higher degree of clustering than can be accounted for by chance.[9]

In other words, humans seem to want to be clustered, even when it's not good for them. But does that mean it's always bad?

Despite how we may currently feel about silos and clusters, recent research suggests that we need some level of clustering and silos to help spread information and opportunity. Damon Centola, a University of Pennsylvania professor and director of the university's Network Dynamics Group, discovered that, quite counterintuitively, breaking down all group boundaries may actually slow the spread of knowledge across a population, not speed it up.[10] Some level of clustering actually makes it easier for best practices, complex ideas, and new opportunities to move across a network.

Using a computational model to assess how ideas and practices spread, Centola was able to vary the level of affiliation that different actors in a network feel for those characteristics they share with others. Put simply, he ran variations of networks where individuals feel more or less attached to people like themselves, and hence networks that are more or less clustered.

What he discovered was that, while reducing the clustering of the network helps ideas to spread, the correlation only holds to a point. When group boundaries and clusters are removed entirely, actors in the network have very little influence on anyone—it becomes a network of near-strangers, and hence ideas and information just don't spread at all. "There's a belief that the more people interact with strangers, the more that new ideas and beliefs will spread," Centola said of his findings. "What this study shows is that preserving group boundaries is actually necessary for complex ideas to become accepted across diverse populations."[11] Centola's findings support the experiences of the Venetian glassmakers and the writers in Paris and Oxford who sought out like-minded people who influenced them and were influenced by them. At the same time, his findings reiterate the warning Ronald Burt issued in his theory of structural holes: staying in a cluster too much can be damaging as well.

In fact, in 2016, Burt himself took up a similar issue when he sought to discover the right way to use clusters to maximize benefits and minimize drawbacks. Burt teamed up with Jennifer Merluzzi, a professor of management at Tulane University, to find the best way to leverage clusters while also being a structural hole.[12] In his work with a large investment bank a number of years earlier, Burt had collected data on 350 of its top-tier bankers. Investment banking is an ideal source of data for this type of experiment since bankers often work in teams on discreet projects, then break up once the project is over. Post-project, different bankers take different approaches to finding a new project. Some just dive right into the next available project team, while others wait, and still others work part-time or consult while waiting for that next perfect assignment.

But eventually, everyone has joined a new, small project team. In other words, some bankers stay inside of small clusters the entire time and then jump right to the next cluster when the project is over, while others oscillate between working in clusters (project teams) and brokering (building bridges to new teams and projects). Burt was able to collect data on who was using which strategy, as well as performance ratings, bonus information, and salaries, for all 350 bankers.

Using this data, Burt and Merluzzi compared which post-project strategy was most effective. They found that bankers who moved between project teams and brokered connections got the most rewards. These bankers spent time in clusters, but they also formed ties in the organization by not jumping into another cluster right away. Instead, they had a wide range of contacts and hence a wider range of opportunity than their clustered counterparts. These brokers "tend to do better than people who only talk to the same set of people with the same set of knowledge," said Merluzzi. "These brokers have gained valuable social capital."[13] And that social capital turned into financial capital too. While the perception of their performance suffered when they weren't locked into a project team, the oscillating bankers collected far more in bonuses and salaries over time.

Burt and Merluzzi's research focused on individual careers inside of one organization, but their findings echo the results of a similar study done across an entire industry almost twenty years prior. When the sociologist Brian Uzzi was a doctoral student (he is now a full professor at the Kellogg School of Management at Northwestern University), he decided to study a network that was already quite close to him: the garment industry. When Uzzi's family immigrated to the United States from Italy, they found their footings in the needle trade, and Uzzi wanted to study it further. He surveyed the garment industry in New York City, first by building out a network based on company information and transactions recorded by the International Ladies' Garment Workers' Union (ILGWU), to which more than 80 percent of the city's apparel company workers belonged.[14] He also conducted interviews with twenty-three companies in that network, often interviewing multiple leaders inside each firm. In total, he collected around 117 hours of interviews on various garment companies' business practices. He also collected data on survival rates—whether or not a company managed to stay in business.

What he found was that New York's garment industry was a vast network, and that everyone managed relationships in that network differently. As Burt and Merluzzi discovered in their research, different individuals had different styles. That is, some preferred to be more clustered and some were more open. Some companies and company leaders chose to do business only with a small circle of trusted allies, what Uzzi labeled "close-knit ties." Others chose to do small amounts of business with a large set of relationships and to keep their relationships purely transactional. Uzzi labeled these "arm's-length ties." Most fell somewhere in between. Just as Centola found in his research on the need for clusters, Uzzi found that having strong close-knit ties enhanced a firm's chances of survival in the industry—that clusters and small circles did seem to help.

But only up to a point.

Eventually, being too clustered and doing business with too few firms had a negative impact on survivability. Uzzi's research revealed that the most successful companies had leaders who maintained a healthy mixture of close-knit and arm's-length ties—whose real-world networks resembled Centola's models. These companies were in a position to choose the best options from among a diverse set of relationships. They had their small circle of allies with whom they could go deep into the relationship, sharing a lot of business and also learning and growing from these relationships, but they also had a collection of distant (let's call them weak) ties with whom they could scan the whole environment and see more opportunities than their more tightly clustered counterparts could.

Taken altogether, this research tells a much different tale about silos and clusters. There's a reason for our tendency toward transitivity—our desire to gravitate toward silos. *Clusters are good for us, and good for our growth.* The trick is to make sure we're not so clustered that we ignore opportunities to be structural holes. At the same time, we need to make certain that pursuing our goals as brokers between clusters doesn't leave us clusterless. Pulling that trick off can be difficult. In many industries, the balance of close-knit groups and arm's-length ties has already been decided. If that's the case in your industry, you might just have to create your own solution.

If You Can't Find Clusters, Create Them

Gertrude Stein's salons not only served to inspire Ernest Hemingway and help him in his development but, almost 100 years later, are still inspiring people to find their own clusters.[15] One such group is the quartet of Elliott Bisnow, Brett Leve, Jeremy Schwartz, and Jeff Rosenthal. In 2008, these four friends and former college classmates were all working as entrepreneurs or for start-ups. While they were happy as a small band of merry innovators, they wanted to expand their circle and also meet other fellow entrepreneurs building interesting companies. To facilitate that, they planned a ski trip and rented a house with space for them and fifteen others. Then they started reaching out. They made a list of dream connections and started cold-calling, emailing, and sometimes even messaging on social media to other young entrepreneurs who inspired them.

It worked. They filled a house in Park City, Utah, with entrepreneurs like Facebook cofounder Dustin Moskovitz, TOMS Shoes founder Blake Mycoskie, charity: water's Scott Harrison, and David Mayer de Rothschild, the environmentalist and explorer who is one of a small number of people ever to visit both the North and South Poles. The four organizers left that surreal ski trip with a resolve to make sure it wasn't a once-in-a-lifetime opportunity. They needed to get the group back together and even expand it. So they planned a follow-up event a few months later. They also asked each of the original guests to invite two friends.

With an expanded guest list, and an even more impressive collection of people, simple momentum took over. They adopted the name Summit Series for their events and developed a brief mission statement of what they were about, which Rosenthal once described as: "Gather people doing innovative work, regardless of their discipline, or just thoughtful, open-minded, kind people we'd want to spend time with, regardless of personal or professional success."[16] Certainly some of the momentum was triggered by the particular collection of people who had attended. But professional success came pretty quickly to Summit, and some of it was simply due to the fact that, at the time, there was no other such gathering place for these individuals. In effect, the four friends had built the kind of cluster that so many entrepreneurs were looking for.

Peter Thiel, a venture capitalist and serial entrepreneur (and a cofounder of PayPal and one of the first people to invest in Facebook) described the value of this new cluster by saying, "The Summit Series team knows that communities of talented people driven to change the world can successfully change it."[17] And despite it being a young community, it already has. By 2009, the Summit team was asked to bring their collection of entrepreneurs to the White House for a meeting between the new leaders of the Obama administration and the existing leaders of the technology start-up world. Summit events were also the catalyst behind several successful start-ups. It was at a Summit event that the founders of Spotify met entrepreneur Sean Parker (of Napster and Facebook). Parker was instrumental in helping Spotify launch in the United States.[18]

In 2011, Summit took to the seas. The team chartered a cruise ship and planned a three-day conference for more than 1,000 young entrepreneurs. The conference, called quite descriptively "Summit at Sea," featured talks from notable entrepreneurs and celebrities, but it was the ship itself that provided the biggest benefit. During the short cruise, everyone had to unplug from their regular lives (the ship was reportedly without wireless Internet for the entire journey) and focus instead on knowing and helping each other. This short-term entry into a cluster was focused on development, followed by going back out into one's own network. The conference logistics almost mirrored the implications of Burt and Merluzzi's study, but the next stage in Summit's evolution provided an even clearer picture.

In April 2013, the Summit team bought a mountain: Powder Mountain in Utah.[19] A Summit attendee had brought it to the attention of the team: "What if Summit Series could literally be at the summit of a mountain?" After researching the opportunity—the ski resort had changed hands a few times as investors struggled to develop it—and gathering investors, the team bought Powder Mountain for $40 million. While it's still being developed, their plan is to build a small town and a members-only lodge. The community will stay small at only around 500 home sites, and most of them will likely be second homes for longtime Summit attendees. But in building the physical community, Summit is re-creating something like Stein and Hemingway's Paris circle: an actual place that houses the needed community. Powder Mountain will allow individual Summit members to leave their everyday network, connect with this clustered community, and then go back out into the world to make an impact—to participate, in effect, in a sort of long-term and recurring Summit at Sea. The end result of the project is not yet known, but the vision is inspiring. Perhaps 100 years from now the iconic story won't be about Stein's Paris salons but about Powder Mountain's ski lodge.

If planning and building a whole town seems like a lot of work just to find the right cluster, then it's possible to start smaller. Instead of 500 home sites and a mountaintop lodge, how about just meeting for coffee once a month? That is what Tina Roth Eisenberg focused on, and she saw her idea grow into a movement in its own right.

In 2008, Eisenberg, a Swiss-born designer, built her own cluster from a simple idea. It's now grown into an international movement that helps give thousands of creative professionals the benefits of community every month.

But let's start at the beginning. Eisenberg moved to New York City in 1999 without any professional or personal contacts in the design industry.[20] That didn't last long. Knowing how important it was to have a cluster of contacts, she started engaging with her professional community by building what she herself needed and what others could benefit from as well. Today she runs Swiss-miss, a hugely popular design blog. She manages TeuxDeux, a productivity app that uses design to focus users on what's important. She founded Tattly, a temporary tattoo company with products created by world-class designers. She's started not one but two coworking spaces. But her great community building project—and the one that's scaled the most by far—is CreativeMornings.

As a professional designer, Eisenberg was fortunate to be able to attend many of the large-scale conferences on the annual design circuit. When she blogged about her experiences, she found that lots of her readers longed to attend these types of events but couldn't for financial reasons, logistical reasons, or some other reason. Even those who did attend longed for something slightly more permanent. "I realized that most of us attend conferences because we want to meet like-minded people," she recalled. "But the problem with conferences is that these communities are temporary and only happen once a year."[21] Eisenberg wanted to build something recurring, and something local.

So she began organizing and hosting a monthly discussion series, which she called CreativeMornings. It started as a solo effort, an attempt to bring creatives in New York City together. After some early trial and error, she settled on a one-morning-a-month format. The events are free to attend, with coffee and a light breakfast paid for by a sponsoring company. The event features a speaker relevant to the community and some discussion, and that's it. Unlike conferences, it's not a multiday event that demands significant time from attendees. Of course, just to be helpful, the CreativeMornings website still features a section aimed at convincing bosses to let their people arrive late on Fridays in order to attend.

It didn't take long for CreativeMornings to spread enthusiastically through New York City. Eventually, hundreds were attending every month, connecting with fellow creatives, and reaping the benefits of clustering while avoiding the negative effects of silos—since every month the community comes together, connects, and then disperses back into the larger industry.

These get-togethers allow attendees to build a mix of arm's-length and close-knit ties as they add new contacts each time but also reconnect with longtime friends—just as Uzzi's earlier study suggests is vital. As word spread nationally, and then internationally, CreativeMornings started enlisting volunteers in other cities to host their own events. Today over 150 cities host monthly CreativeMornings events. As a global community, CreativeMornings sets a theme for the month and encourages meeting organizers in every city to find a speaker who addresses that theme. Every month thousands of people throughout those cities meet and connect through the ideas arising out of that theme. "It's like a global conversation with all these chapters," Eisenberg said.[22]

Eisenberg didn't envision this global community when she started. In fact, at times she figured it was just going to be a regular coffee appointment once a month for her and a few friends. But today she cites CreativeMornings as the biggest achievement in her career. It's now grown beyond her control into a global movement precisely because it provides the same key element she herself was looking for by starting it: access to a community that meets frequently enough to be meaningful and makes no overwhelming demands. "What I was craving was an accessible event, that connects me with my local creative community, and that inspires me with one talk—before work," she explained.[23] Apparently, so were thousands of others across the globe.

The Summit Series team and Tina Roth Eisenberg stumbled upon the same discoveries made by Hemingway and Stein, Lewis and The Inklings, and the glassmakers of Murano. Rather than being trapped, they all found that being in a small cluster—part of a small group of similar people—can be vital for growth and development. Likewise, the research suggests that industry networks and geographic communities benefit as well from faster knowledge-sharing when some level of clustering is in the mix. However, the trick is to not get so comfortable inside a cluster that we become stuck in that silo. Finding a real and meaningful balance between deep community and wide networks is vital for professional success. We need clusters to help develop our skills and knowledge so that we can have an impact that resonates across the network.

FROM SCIENCE TO PRACTICE

Despite the widespread warnings in the modern business literature about silos, research suggests that having a regular cluster with whom you interact, share, learn, grow, and develop is a vital part of a successful career. The most connected, most successful individuals oscillate between working with a variety of teams and acting as bridges from their primary team to elsewhere in the organization or network.

Like Gertrude Stein's Paris salons that helped Hemingway, or the Summit Series events that inspire modern entrepreneurs, you need to be plugged into a community that you can grow in. If you don't have a team that you can interact with briefly but regularly, it's time to be like so many in this chapter and just start your own. Here's how:

1. Make a list of ten to fifteen people who work in your profession or do something similar enough to have shared experiences. These can be people you know already or people who would respond to a cold invitation to be a part of your cluster. (If reaching out with cold invitations to strangers or mere acquaintances, it's better to have commitments from a few contacts already so that the group is already a certainty.)
2. Commit to a regular interval of meetings. Once a month is a good starting place, but you can adjust the regularity depending on the people in your cluster.
3. Commit to a set structure for your conversations. This doesn't have to be a rigid agenda, but it's good to have a map to follow in each meeting so that no one feels their time is wasted. If you don't know where to start, consider asking

these three questions and going around to each member of the cluster for answers:

- *What are you working on right now? What project is top of mind and dominating your time right now?* This gives everyone in the cluster a sense of each person's priorities.
- *What is holding you back? In other words, how can the group help you?* Maybe the group can help with advice, access to resources, introductions, or something else entirely. Spending time on this question helps ensure that everyone leaves each meeting with something valuable.
- *What do you need prompting on? What can we do to keep you accountable?* Everyone has projects or tasks they know they need to do but forget about from day to day or week to week. One of the benefits of enlisting a team is that they can remind you to check those items off your list each time the team meets—making it harder for them to hide from your attention.

For the first few meetings, you may need to act as a moderator to keep everyone on task. Likewise, you may find that the questions you ask change or the overall agenda is revised. That is okay. The important thing is that you've found and built a community that you can turn to regularly for growth and accountability. And bonus points if you can come up with a clever name like the "The Inklings" for your cluster.

Practicing Online

While ideally every meeting would happen in person, often travel schedules or geographic locations can make that difficult. Fortunately, there is a vast collection of tools online that can help make virtual meetings a reality. From video conferencing programs to the small-groups features on most social media services, you and your cluster have a lot to choose from. (Because the technology and software worlds change so frequently, I've included a regularly updated list of tools in the downloadable template at http://davidburkus.com/resources/.) If you do hold some of your meetings virtually, it's still a good idea to commit to a regular cycle of in-person meetings. Even if it's only once a year or once a quarter, being face to actual face is an important element of growing the trust and commitment of group members.

For a downloadable template to use when completing this exercise, go to http://davidburkus.com/resources/ and look for networking resources.

— 5 —

BUILD TEAMS FROM ALL OVER YOUR NETWORK

Or
Why the Best Teams Don't Stay Together Long

Knowing that clusters and collaboration are important, we can easily assume that the best teams are those that have stuck together for a long time—those that have performed well again and again. But research offers a different lesson, revealing that many of the most successful teams are successful only because they are temporary—they meet for a time and then disband, with some members going to other teams. In the end, having a large network and a tight-knit team isn't as valuable as having a loose network and temporary teams.

IN THE SUMMER OF 2005, a few friends in the Silicon Valley area got together for a backyard barbecue—one of many that probably happened that day across that region of California and across the country.[1] This barbecue, however, would end up being a milestone event that led to a dramatic change in the history of technology and in the way individuals interact online. During the get-together, Jawed Karim, a then-twenty-six-year-old computer science programmer, showed a website he was working on to Keith Rabois, a man ten years his senior. Rabois was impressed with the website and told another friend, Roelof Botha, who happened to be a partner at the venture capital firm Sequoia Capital.

Botha, also impressed, arranged a meeting with Karim and the other men working on the project. A few months later, Sequoia had invested $3.5 million in the new website.[2] Just a few weeks after that, the website officially launched for all to use, even though over 8 million people were already visiting it daily.

Post-launch, the website would soar. Within a year of the first investment from Sequoia, the search engine powerhouse Google jumped in and purchased the website for $1.65 billion.[3] The website, YouTube.com, would continue its rocketlike trajectory even after purchase, eventually becoming the second most visited website in the world.[4] From the backyard cookout to the Google buyout, Karim and his friends had taken YouTube from a one-video demo website to a $1.65 billion company in just eighteen months. Needless to say, the investment from Sequoia Capital helped them get there, and it helped Sequoia make a substantial profit. It seems like an amazing fantasy story, a near-fluke, except that YouTube isn't the only company that has received significant investment based on a small idea. It's not the only company to go from idea to billion-dollar valuation in less than two years. It's not even the only company that got its lucky break at a small backyard get-together.

The truth is, those kinds of things happen all the time when the mafia gets together.

No, not that mafia. The PayPal Mafia.

Jawed Karim and his YouTube cofounders, Steve Chen and Chad Hurley, along with friend Keith Rabois and venture capitalist Roelof Botha, all worked together at the financial start-up PayPal before it was acquired by eBay for $1.5 billion in 2002. But they aren't the entire PayPal Mafia, not even a majority. Other members include Peter Thiel, Elon Musk, Reid Hoffman, Andrew McCormack, David Sacks, Ken Howery, Max Levchin, Russel Simmons, and a few hundred more. (There is a debate about just how many people count as the PayPal Mafia, but former PayPal CEO Peter Thiel estimates the group at around 220.)[5] The "mafia" label had floated around Silicon Valley for a while before being solidified in a 2007 *Fortune* article on the group.

The companies the Mafia has started or invested in are renowned, including LinkedIn, Yelp, Yammer, Keva, Palantir, Slide, Flickr, Digg, Mozilla, Tesla, SpaceX, and even Facebook.[6] It's an incredible story not just of how start-up genius loves company, but of how those individuals who are plugged into a network can have a dramatic effect on not just their own careers but an entire industry.

The PayPal Mafia got its start, of course, at PayPal. Founded by Max Levchin, Luke Nosek, and Peter Thiel, PayPal started to send mobile payments from person to person using Palm Pilots and other personal digital assistants (and originally carried the name Confinity). From the beginning, the company focused on recruiting through its founders' networks and then building a company where everyone felt connected. That meant heavy recruiting from nearby Stanford University (Thiel's alma mater) and also from the University of Illinois at Urbana-Champaign (Levchin's alma mater). "We didn't only hire our friends," said Thiel. "But we did hire people who we thought we could become really good friends with."[7]

Within a few years, the company had pivoted to offering a means to send payments via email and found success as a trusted transaction partner on the eBay auction platform. But PayPal wasn't the only company rushing to make peer-to-peer electronic payments a reality. In the summer of 2001, PayPal merged with X.com, a start-up founded by Elon Musk. Musk had started X.com with the money from selling his first company, Zip2, and he envisioned building an all-inclusive financial portal where users could manage not just their checking and savings accounts but also their retirement and investment needs. That all-inclusive portal included a means to send money to friends electronically, and soon X.com and Confinity had realized it was better to join forces than to fight each other. In an interesting quirk of history, both companies actually leased space in the same office complex for a time before the merger, and when PayPal moved to new offices, X.com expanded into its old space.

Despite the fast growth, or most likely because of it, it was not all smooth sailing. The company fought with regulators, fought with hostile credit card companies, fought off fraudsters and thieves, and even had to fight competition from eBay, its biggest source of users. There were internal fights as well. Disagreements could even turn physical and result in wrestling matches.[8] The CEO position at the company was wrestled over for a time. Post-merger, the company was led by Bill Harris, who resigned quickly after a dispute over strategy with Musk; subsequently, Musk took the reins. Musk, though, was fired by the board over a dispute about technology, and Peter Thiel then became CEO.

These fights eventually gave way to a common enemy, and a surprising one at that. To compete with PayPal, eBay had purchased a money transfer company and was making strategic moves to eliminate PayPal from its platform. PayPal battled back, both by improving its product and by rallying support from eBay's users. At a June 2002 eBay user conference, PayPal threw a party and gave everyone who attended blue PayPal shirts to wear for the conference. Amid a sea of blue, eBay's senior leadership must have seen the light. A month later, eBay announced that it was purchasing PayPal.

While the acquisition worked out well financially for PayPal employees, it didn't work out as well culturally. PayPal was already a misfit in the Silicon Valley culture of the late 1990s and early 2000s—a time when start-up mythology wasn't as prominent as it is today. PayPal's culture was a precursor to the "move fast and break things" ideology that companies in the region would later become known for. At the time it acquired PayPal, eBay was a large company with a team of professional managers—a culture that the PayPal folks found to be a stuffy bureaucracy. From the very beginning of the integration, the PayPal folks were beginning to question how long they would stick around.

For instance, early on in the integration, eBay leaders scheduled a three-hour-long meeting and arrived with a 137-slide PowerPoint deck. "In the history of PayPal, there has never been a three hour meeting, period," said Keith Rabois, a former executive vice president at PayPal. "And they started off the integration meeting with a three hour time block."[9] Within a few months, a number of the founding team members had left. Eventually, nearly half of PayPal's 200-something employees had left and gone elsewhere. Just 12 of the first 50 employees at PayPal were still there four years after the acquisition.[10] "With PayPal, you essentially had this mass exodus of highly entrepreneurial people who had learned all these techniques, that were very innovative, that could make a new product explode, at a time when everybody else had given up," said David Sacks, the former chief operating officer of PayPal.[11]

And making new products explode is exactly what they did.

Almost immediately after cashing out from the sale, Peter Thiel founded the hedge fund Clarium Capital, where he was joined by PayPal veterans Andrew McCormack and Ken Howery. Thiel would also become the first outside investor in a fledgling start-up called Facebook, getting his friend and former PayPal coworker Reid Hoffman involved. It wouldn't be Reid Hoffman's only social network either. After his exit, Hoffman and a few others started LinkedIn, which quickly accepted investment money from Keith Rabois and Peter Thiel. Another member of the PayPal Mafia even provided the space for LinkedIn's first office.[12] Even Elon Musk, who took his earnings from the sale and founded Tesla Motors and SpaceX, still relied on help from the PayPal Mafia for ideas and funding. When Musk's attempt at building a more cost-efficient space rocket failed three straight times and seriously drained his funding for SpaceX, it was a former colleague from PayPal who invested enough to keep him experimenting.[13]

One reason for their tight-knit circle of new start-ups was the set of friendships that remained from their PayPal days. But another factor that dramatically strengthened those bonds was the economy. In the early 2000s, when the colleagues went from being eBay employees to free agents, very little money was flowing to consumer-based technology start-ups. "Nobody would fund them," said Keith Rabois. "Basically, there was just Reid [Hoffman], Peter [Thiel], and a few of us, as well as Sequoia to some extent."[14] But the PayPal Mafia didn't just control the money, they also shaped the ideas. Because most of the new companies started by PayPal refugees also featured new members, the philosophy and culture of the PayPal Mafia spread. Even where the Mafia didn't directly work with a new company but merely invested in it, their influence was still strong. Part of what explains the culture and ethos of Silicon Valley today is the very clear impression the PayPal Mafia left on each new venture they touched. After several billion-dollar companies and tens of billions of dollars in market capitalization, it's safe to say that impression was positive. In sum, a rogue band of misfits, driven out by eBay, became the central nodes for a strong network of astounding innovation.

But it's not just the former relationships and their considerable wealth to invest that explain the success of the PayPal Mafia. Recent research into how network connections best interact suggests that it's the specific way in which the PayPal Mafia collaborated that now explains their success.

The Best Collaborations Are Temporary

In the early 2000s, Brian Uzzi took an interest in how top-performing teams find each other and collaborate—specifically, how the social networks of their respective industries affected the people who found and collaborated with each other. At first, Uzzi was just looking at the realm of science, but his investigations would span a variety of domains. In science, for example, Uzzi and his colleagues found that scientific breakthroughs were increasingly becoming a team affair. In one study, Uzzi, along with researchers Stefan Wuchty and Benjamin Jones, found that the rate at which expanding collaborations were resulting in impactful scientific papers was rising quickly. The researchers gathered nearly 20 million peer-reviewed papers and over 2 million patents published between 1955 and 2000.[15] What they found was a steady increase—almost a doubling—in the number of people on collaborative teams. In 1955, for example, the average team size for a published paper was just 1.9 people, reflecting a strong tendency at the time for researchers to work alone. Five decades later, the average team size had grown to 3.5.

The amount of solo work versus team work that scientists engaged in also changed. Looking at social scientists in particular, in the 1950s they wrote only 17.5 percent of their papers on teams; fifty years later that percentage had grown to 51.5 percent. In other words, fifty years ago the image of the genius working alone in a lab was fairly accurate. But today the majority of genius is applied through extended teamwork.

Uzzi's research trio also found an upward trend in the impact of team work on a field compared to solo work. The best way to judge impact is by the number of citations—how many future papers reference a particular paper is often used as a proxy for the quality and impact of its research. Over the fifty-year period studied, coauthored papers were cited more often than solo-authored ones, and the percentage of coauthored papers cited grew. In the 1950s, coauthored papers received 1.7 times the number of citations as individually written papers received. By 2000, they were receiving 2.1 times as many citations. Even after controlling for self-citations (scientists citing their own work in future papers), the impact of coauthored papers, and the strong growth of that impact, remained intact.

The rise of discovery as a team sport naturally leads to a follow-up question: what makes for the best teams?

Luckily, Uzzi and a different team of researchers (a significant detail that will be explained in a moment) have looked into that as well. This team of researchers pulled a much smaller data set of scientific papers published between 1955 and 2004.[16] This smaller set was still pretty large, representing almost 90,000 papers and 115,000 authors in 32 journals from a variety of scientific fields. Uzzi, along with Roger Guimerà, Luís Amaral, and Jarrett Spiro, were particularly interested in the frequency of repeat collaborations. Does genius insight result from a small group of scientists working together for a long time . . . or does it stem from *temporary* collaborations? (As suggested, Uzzi's own research in this area suggests his faith in the latter possibility, as each paper he has coauthored resulted from a slightly different collaboration.)

To examine this question, the researchers also needed to assess the quality of the papers, for which they used the impact of the journal in which each paper was published as a proxy. Surprisingly, repeat collaborations were more common in low-impact journals. In high-impact journals, it was much more common to see papers by coauthors who had never worked together before and who would go on to join different teams once the paper was published. *The best teams appeared to be only temporary.*

Part of the explanation for this finding lies in the nature of scientific research. From the initial hypothesis to the data collection to the manuscript preparation, a lot of work goes into publishing a scientific paper. It's not just a brilliant theory that makes an impact. It's a brilliant theory supported by mountains of data. The best chance to accomplish that is often found in building a team of high-status individuals with a proven track record of good ideas balanced with relative newcomers, who may be short on experience but are long on the time and energy needed to invest in the project.

But here's the frustrating part: finding a good team and then sticking with it often yields a diminishing return on investment. That is, if a team's first projects are successful, it is less likely to have as much time and energy to devote to the next project. In effect, *you need fresh blood*. And to get that, you need a network that allows individuals not only to come together quickly but also to bring in enough new collaborators to sustain a project.

It turns out that this effect—temporary teams forming across a network of talent—isn't just limited to the sciences.

Consider how the members of the PayPal Mafia didn't just form a new company upon exiting eBay. Instead, they dispersed throughout the technology community, found new collaborators, and benefited from connections to ideas and resources that their old coworkers provided. It wasn't having a group of tried-and-true technology innovators that mattered as much as their dispersal through the network to form new companies. "The rotation of team personnel is critical to creativity," Uzzi explained. "Even if it comes at the loss of efficient communication among team members that have come to know each other and their work habits well."[17]

For the members of the PayPal Mafia, their new situation post-acquisition forced them to find new teams and to rotate around on various projects. In fact, it wasn't uncommon to see a Mafia member join a team of a few former colleagues and new entrepreneurs, work for a short tour of duty, and then jump ship to yet another project. Many even worked on multiple projects at once, founding one company, investing in another, and serving as an adviser to a third. The arrangements of PayPal Mafia members throughout the network of Silicon Valley looks a lot like the collaborations of scientific researchers.

For individuals, the implications of the PayPal Mafia's successes are as clear as they are counterintuitive. It's not enough to merely have a network . . . it's the density of that network that matters. Recall from the previous chapter that finding clusters and collaborators is hugely important. If your network allows you to form teams of new and old connections easily, you have a great blend. If it doesn't, you are probably working too often with the same old people. At the same time, if every project or opportunity requires new rounds of introductions, then the shape of your network isn't optimal.

For organizations, the implications are a little more serious. Most companies are built on organizational charts that set up distinct barriers to collaboration—exactly the *opposite* of what's needed for effective collaboration. Instead of a hierarchy, most organizations would be better served by an organizational structure built like a network of scientific collaborators, with PayPal Mafia–level density.

Making Organizational Charts into Fluid Networks

For most organizations, the organizational chart determines the network. As a company grows and expands, it becomes impossible for everyone to meet and work alongside everyone else. So naturally, reporting relationships are developed. People are grouped and herded by specialization and usually assigned a manager to report to. While the speed of communication up and down the hierarchy generally increases, the speed of communication *horizontally* typically slows to a near-halt. Even worse, the odds of anyone finding new collaborators on a project team become almost nonexistent. Teams in general become defined as "people who report to the same manager," and rotating team members becomes unnatural. Some companies, however, have actually managed to make the rotation of talent and diversity into the norm, not the exception.

IDEO, the internationally renowned design consultancy, stands out as a perfect example. The company was founded in 1991 out of a merger of three design studios.[18] David Kelley, one of the founders and still one of the chief figureheads of the company, often claimed that he started the company with one goal: to create a workplace made up of his best friends.[19] He also claimed that he wanted the company to never grow past forty people, presumably to keep that "working with friends" feeling. But the company did grow, and rapidly. It experienced some very public successes early on, such as designing the first computer mouse for Apple Computers, creating a twenty-five-foot mechanical whale for the movie *Free Willy*, and being featured on an episode of ABC's *Nightline* in which they showcased their entire creative process and redesigned the standard shopping cart. The company also won more industry awards than any other design firm throughout the 1990s. Success brought more success, which brought more work—which required growth.

Today IDEO has offices around the world and employs more than 650 people.[20] The company's growth has made it difficult to keep that "small company, working with friends" feeling, but one of the primary ways they continue to achieve it is by designing their organizational chart around projects instead of around people. As new client projects come in, IDEO builds the team for each project from scratch. The teams themselves are highly diverse, combining engineers with architects, psychologists with anthropologists.[21] The diverse mix of backgrounds provides a level of diversity and creativity that most firms only dream about attaining, but it's the unique nature of IDEO's organizational structure—which allows teams to come together, perform, and disband to join new teams—that is one of the real keys to its creative success.

Since the teams are built specifically for each project, and every new project is different, every team is different. But great things happen because every team combines talented designers with other specialists. "IDEOers are so smart and talented that when a new project comes in, we can put together a seemingly random team of designers out of who is available at that time," David Kelley explained. "And in the end, magic happens: breakthrough ideas and happy clients."[22]

IDEO's process for building teams might seem random, but

it's hardly that. IDEO uses a social platform to pick the perfect people for each team.[23] All IDEO employees have profiles on the platform, which is rich with information about their education, capabilities, and past performance on projects. The profiles are shared across the entire company and can be searched and tagged electronically. The platform provides a quick and effective means for finding the right teammates from a broader pool than just one person's past collaborators. And it also works in reverse—that is, employees can use the platform to search out opportunities for new projects that match their skill sets and their interests.

The unique nature of IDEO's work and its unique approach to building teams make its organizational chart look a lot like the PayPal Mafia network of Silicon Valley—except it's all internal. When a new project comes in, a new team is built from a pool of those who are in the system and available. The project lasts for a few months, and then the team is disbanded and its members go back into the broader network of IDEO employees to await the next assignment. (Often they are already working in some capacity on the next assignment by the time the team disbands.) When employees find their next project, they are on a new team with new faces—and a few old ones.

Whether it's the large-scale network of the PayPal Mafia, a scientific laboratory, or the offices of a design firm like IDEO, the lesson is that the best networks allow fluid teams to form. So many of us approach building a network by searching for trusted individuals with whom we'll work forever. We tend to assume that the best teams are ones that have held fast together for a long time. But the hard research on the nature of teams and networks suggests that the best and most productive teams are only temporary.

FROM SCIENCE TO PRACTICE

The lesson of networks of collaboration is that the best team for working on a project or even just providing advice is temporary —one that probably works together for less time than you would think necessary to be truly effective. To get that team, however, you need a network that's loose and diverse enough to build or rebuild a new roster frequently. The best way to judge whether you have that network is to audit your calendar and see how you are currently interacting with teams of people. Here is a quick but powerful way to evaluate your team meetings and decide whether your network is too tight to form the teams you need:

1. Look back over your calendar for the last three months and list any project meetings you attended.
2. For each meeting, write down the names of everyone who attended the meeting. This list might get long; if a project team meets regularly, then you may be rewriting everyone's name each time.
3. As you build the list, put an asterisk (*) next to the name of anyone you are working on multiple teams with.
4. Next, put a plus symbol (+) next to the name of anyone who is also serving on multiple teams you meet with (meaning two different teams have both you and that person on them).

Once your list is complete, determine what percentage of teammates on the total list are serving on multiple teams. While this may be a somewhat arbitrary cutoff, it's a major red flag if more than half of the people on your list serve on multiple teams. Ideally, even if you're serving on only one main project team, different meetings should be held to draw and attract new attendees from your network or the networks of others. Another red flag is if the same people are meeting in the same room on a regular basis.

Practicing Online

It's an older technology, but you may find it easier to complete this list by leveraging the original social media: email. Use your saved, deleted, and sent emails to get a better idea of who was in what meeting. Even better, if you or your organization uses a calendar service like Outlook or Google Calendar, you have access to a thorough record of who else was invited to those meetings and who at least said they would attend. (It's up to you to remember who was actually there.)

For a downloadable template to use when completing this exercise, go to http://davidburkus.com/resources/ and look for networking resources.

— 6 —

BECOME A SUPER-CONNECTOR

Or
Why Some People Really Do Know Everybody

When we look out at our network and the networks of others, it's easy to assume that all our networks are around the same size. Research into human networks, however, reveals that some people have drastically more connections than whatever would be an average — they are super-connectors. But the evidence also suggests that most of us have the ability to grow our network large enough to become a super-connector. We just need to grow it carefully.

BRIAN GRAZER WASN'T BORN well connected. But he was born curious. And that curiosity led him to become a successful producer and a super-connector. Or perhaps the more appropriate order is that his curiosity led him to be a super-connector, and that in turn led him to become a successful producer.

Through his firm, Imagine Entertainment, Grazer has produced blockbuster films such as *Apollo 13*, *Liar Liar*, *A Beautiful Mind*, and *8 Mile* and television shows such as *Arrested Development* and *24*. But Brian's original plan was never to work in

Hollywood, and certainly not as a producer. His curiosity and his connections led him there.

Grazer was originally supposed to go to law school. He graduated from the University of Southern California and was set to continue to USC School of Law, but one fateful summer day he overhead a conversation that changed his life. "I overheard two guys talking," Grazer reflected. "One said, 'Oh my God, I had the cushiest job at Warner Bros. I got paid for eight hours of work every day, and it was usually just an hour.'"[1] Intrigued, Grazer listened more closely and learned that the speaker had just quit his job as a law clerk, and he even overheard the name of the man's former boss.

Curious and also assertive, Grazer looked up the number for Warner Bros., called, and asked for the man's former boss. Grazer said he was a law student and was looking for a summer job. The boss asked if they could meet at 3:00 p.m. the next day. "He hired me at 3:15. I started at Warner Bros. the next Monday," Grazer recalled.[2]

He quickly learned that the job did indeed involve very little work, but that it also had very little gravitas. Grazer was given a windowless room, barely the size of a closet, but it was a start. "From that tiny office, I joined the world of show business. I never again worked at anything else," Grazer reflected.[3] From those humble beginnings, Grazer developed his passion for the industry. And they were humble. The title may have been "law clerk," but in fact he was nothing more than a courier. His job was to deliver documents, contracts, and other material to people working on Warner Bros. projects. The job was simple and boring: He was given an address. He would drop off the papers, and that was it. It would have been depressing if not for Grazer's never-ending curiosity and determination to make it all fun.

"I realized I'm delivering these papers to very, very famous people, but they also had people between themselves and me," Grazer explained.[4] So Grazer decided to do something to work around those people. "When I showed up, I would tell the intermediary—the secretary, the doorman—that I had to hand the documents directly to the person for the delivery to be 'valid.'"[5] Surprisingly, it worked. No one really questioned him.

Grazer soon started meeting powerful executives and film actors, and many of them would even invite him in for a quick chat. He met Oscar-winning directors like Billy Friedkin. He met movie stars like Warren Beatty. From there he would learn a bit more about the movie business or get some career advice. "Pretty quick, I realized the movie business was a lot more interesting than law school," Grazer explained. "So I put it off—I never went." Instead, he dedicated himself to learning more and more from these conversations and started to build a career for himself in Hollywood. To do that, he needed to get more advice. And to do that, he needed to get closer to the action.

As luck would have it, around the same time he had this revelation, a senior vice president at Warner Bros. was fired and vacated his office. The office he left was right next to the executive suite of offices, where the president, chairman, and vice chairman of the studio worked. Grazer took a gamble and made a simple request to work out of that office while it was empty. "Sure," his boss said, and he arranged the move. Grazer was just a simple law clerk, but he was working out of an important office—and even had his own secretary. Importantly, the office was next to John Calley, the vice chairman of Warner Bros., who quickly took a liking to Grazer and invited him to sit in his office often. Grazer quickly learned more about the movie business, but he also developed an even bolder idea for growing his assortment of connections.

"I realized I didn't have to meet only the people Warner Bros.

happened to be doing business with that day," Grazer recalled. If he structured his request properly, he figured he could probably get a meeting with pretty much anyone in the business. He could simply call and ask for an appointment, and if he was persistent, he would eventually get one. So he developed a brief pitch and starting dialing. He would call the assistants of powerful executives and give them a well-rehearsed but simple ask: "Hi, my name is Brian Grazer. I work for Warner Bros. Business Affairs. This is not associated with studio business, and I do not want a job, but I would like to meet Mr. So-and-So for five minutes to talk to him." Then he would finish with a specific reason why he was interested and why meeting with him would be worth the person's time.[6]

Just like his speech when delivering legal documents, Grazer's new pitch worked more often than not. He met producers from other studios, he met directors, and each time he left with useful information and the name of someone else to meet. "Talking to one person in the movie business suggested a half dozen more people I could talk to," Grazer reflected. "Each success gave me the confidence to try for the next person. It turned out I really could talk to almost anyone in the business."[7]

Sometimes it would take repeated efforts to get a meeting, but those meetings were almost always worth it. One such long-awaited conversation was Grazer's first sit-down with Lew Wasserman. Wasserman was the head of MCA, the studio that would eventually become NBCUniversal. Through MCA, Wasserman had worked with movie stars like Judy Garland, Fred Astaire, and Jimmy Stewart, and he had even worked with Alfred Hitchcock. At the time Grazer was seeking him out, Wasserman was the most powerful man in movies.

Wasserman met Grazer for only ten minutes, but his advice would shape Grazer's career forever. "Go write something," Wasserman told him. "You have to bring the idea."[8] As great as his conversations were, and as numerous as his contacts were becoming, Grazer needed to use those contacts to develop ideas . . . otherwise he would never become a producer.

It was this search that ultimately led Grazer to his lifelong business partner, Ron Howard.

Grazer first saw Howard on the lot at Paramount Studios, where he was working as a producer on smaller projects like television movies. Similar to his strategy for reaching out to just about anyone, Grazer called Howard and just said, "I think we have similar goals. Let's meet and talk about it."[9] A few days later, they met in person and discussed their goals of working on mainstream media, and a partnership was born. They did two movies together at first, and when one of them, *Splash,* became a hit, they formed their own company, Imagine Entertainment. They have been working together ever since. "My relationship with Ron has been the most important in my life, outside of my family," Grazer reflected. "He's my closest work colleague, and my best friend."[10]

But his longtime partnership with Howard hasn't stopped Grazer from continuing to cultivate new connections. He's still seeking out new people to have what he calls "curiosity conversations." For more than thirty-five years, he's made conversations with interesting people a regular part of his routine. "My goal was always at least one every two weeks," he explained. Just to name a few: He's met President Bill Clinton and scientist Carl Sagan. He's met vaccine inventor Jonas Salk and billionaire Carlos Slim. He's met rapper 50 Cent and oceanographer Jacques Cousteau.[11] He even met Princess Diana—and shared a bowl of ice cream with her.[12]

A good number of Grazer's meetings have been deliberately outside of the world of movies and television, but many of them have influenced his ideas for new shows and new movies. In addition, he's pretty much met everyone he needs to know inside the movie business. Knowing them is part of his everyday job as a producer. "Work means meetings with actors, writers, directors, musicians. The phone calls—with agents, producers, studio heads, stars—start well before I reach the office, and often follow me home," Grazer said. In many ways, that is the job of a producer—to be the hub that connects all of these different groups working on a film or a television show. For that reason, his desire to know as large and diverse a set of people as possible is no doubt one of the major contributors to his success. Grazer is a super-connector. He's one of a small group of individuals in a social network who amass a collection of contacts that is shockingly larger than average. And for Grazer at least, the size of that collection explains the size of his success.

Above-Average Networks (Far Above Average)

If Brian Grazer's story seems like an anomaly, it's because it is . . . at least compared to our mental model of how big someone's network should be. Most of us assume that other people have networks about the same size as our own—that because we can only keep so many relationships in our head, everyone has around the same number of connections. We may think that a few "lucky ones" have a more powerful collection of contacts, but it's doubtful (we assume) that they know more people than average. They were just dealt a better hand. When we do think about those super-connectors with abnormally large networks, we reassure ourselves that they must not know everyone as closely as we know the people in our network. And there's a good scientific argument around that idea.

The origins of that argument belong to Robin Dunbar, an evolutionary psychologist from the University of Oxford. In the early 1990s, Dunbar was studying the social connections among groups of primates—monkeys and apes mostly.[13] Through his observations, Dunbar worked up a theory that the size of the groups observed must have been influenced by the size of the animals' brains. It takes brainpower to interact with other animals, to socialize and bond with them and remember past interactions. So by extension, how many of those interactions a primate can keep straight must correlate to how much brainpower the animal has. That, in turn, must correlate to how large the animal's brain is—specifically to the animal's neocortex.

This led Dunbar to another conclusion. If the size of the neocortex plays a role in limiting the social circles of primates, then this must extrapolate out to humans. "Since the size of the human neocortex is known, the relationship between group size and neocortex size in primates can be used to predict the cognitive group size for humans," Dunbar and his colleague Russell Hill wrote.[14]

Using the known average size of a human neocortex, Dunbar calculated the upper limit of a human's information-processing capacity and brainpower to socialize in a network at around 150 contacts. This became known in scientific and popular literature as *Dunbar's number*. Dunbar then went looking for evidence of this number in human social groups. He studied anthropological field reports from tribal societies and modern ones and (along with Hill) even studied the average numbers of Christmas cards sent by individuals every year. Each time he saw this average of around 150. Elsewhere, 150 was also the typical size of military units in the Roman Empire and of infantry units during World War I.[15] There's evidence that modern businesses and military groups still tend to divide their units up at around 150, though this is an average and the deviation from the mean varies widely.

But there is a problem with Dunbar's number when it comes to estimating the size of a particular human's social network—two problems really. The first is that Dunbar's research mostly focused on the tribes and groups of nonhumans (monkeys and apes) and then extrapolated that data to estimate an average for humans. The bigger problem, however, is that 150 just doesn't seem to be the right number. Moreover, the real number may shatter our concept of "average."

In 2010, a trio of researchers led by Tyler McCormick, then a PhD student in statistics at Columbia University, attempted to estimate the average size of an individual's network using surveys and statistical calculations in lieu of brain size.[16] Measuring the size of an individual's collection of contacts is difficult, for a variety of reasons. Researchers cannot just ask how big someone's network is. Nor can they just scroll through the address book on each participant's smartphone. To get a more accurate count, McCormick and his colleagues tested a variety of methods, all of which used specific prompts to trigger known contacts. In this case, they asked 1,370 adults in the United States how many people they knew with certain first names (for example, "How many Michaels do you know? How many Jennifers?"). This technique prompted individuals to remember specific people, and the results could be compared to widely available data on how many people share specific names. (In the United States, the Social Security Administration keeps data on names of newborns by year.) Using a few statistical calculations, the researchers could then arrive at an estimate of network size for each individual.

They found that the average (mean) network size of those surveyed was 611 people. Taken by itself, this number is dramatically larger than Dunbar's estimate. But another insight hidden in the data is even more dramatic. While the *mean* network size was 611 contacts, the *median* was 472 contacts. This difference might not seem like a big deal to you or me, but to a statistician it's a clear signal. The assumption in Dunbar's research was that not only was the average network size around 150, but that if drawn on a graph, the results would follow what is known as a *normal distribution*. In a normal distribution, you tend to have a line climbing from the beginning of the graph, reaching a peak in the middle, and then tapering back down. This is the bell curve, or upside-down U shape, that many of us are familiar with from high school mathematics.

In a normal distribution, you would also see the median network size equal the average (the mean). Real human network sizes actually might be four times larger than Dunbar's estimate, but if 611 people is the average and the distribution is normal, it should also be the median. This wasn't the case with the results that McCormick and his colleagues arrived at, and, in fact, those results indicated an entirely different shape to the graph.

To them, network sizes looked more similar to a *power law*.

A power law is a different kind of distribution. Instead of a bell curve, a power law looks like the steepest hill you have ever seen. It starts high and then drops quickly before almost leveling off near the horizontal axis. (In a pure power law, neither point of the line would touch the axes, but real samples tend to look a little messier.) Indeed, this is what McCormick and his colleagues found. While a lot of people had network sizes around 600 people, a few had dramatically larger networks. Those few people with massive networks skewed the distribution into this power law shape.

To be fair to Dunbar, he did hedge his bets when it came to calculating the number. He actually allowed for a few different numbers, which increased with orders of magnitude as the list of contacts became less intimate. In each case, however, he also assumed that there was an upper limit to how many contacts any one person could have in their network. There may well be an upper limit, *but it's nowhere near the average.*

McCormick and his colleagues are not the only people studying the presence of power laws in networks. They are not even the first. Credit for that discovery goes to Albert-László Barabási and Réka Albert. As early as the mid-1990s, Barabási and Albert were studying networks, both person-to-person and technological networks like the world wide web.[17] Because they were studying webpages on the Internet in addition to personal networks, they had noticed fairly early on that many websites, nodes in the network, had very large collections of hyperlinks compared to other webpages. As the world wide web evolved, certain places became the preferred starting point for Internet users, and over time these websites were linked to much more frequently than average. In addition, many of these websites happened to be linking to the large collections of other websites. (In the early days of the Internet, websites like Yahoo.com and Excite.com tried to act as a front door to the Internet, linking to a diverse array of other informational websites.) To the researchers, it was fairly easy to see that the pattern didn't follow an assumed normal distribution—instead, it followed a power law.

This led them to wonder if the same phenomenon held true for human networks. They chose the Hollywood data set from the now-infamous "six degrees of Kevin Bacon" studies. When they graphed the level of connectivity in the actor network of Hollywood, a power law again emerged: there was certainly an average number of connections, but a small subset of actors were dramatically more connected than the norm. In fact, these extremely well-connected actors were what allowed the small-world effect to happen. Not only were they well connected, but they kept everyone else much more closely connected than they would otherwise have been.

Over time these key individuals (or nodes when speaking of a nonhuman network) became known as super-connectors—not only do they possess super-collections of contacts, but they keep everyone in the network super-connected. Consider Brian Grazer as a super-connector; the importance of his vast collection of individuals to his work is readily apparent. Now he regularly interacts with a diverse set of individuals outside of Hollywood, but because of his early work in getting to know almost everyone in the movie business, he is a super-connector for the industry. Since much of the work of a producer is keeping various parties on a project connected and working together, being a super-connector has made him a super producer. His collection of contacts and conversation is rivaled only by his collection of Oscar and Emmy nominations.

But as we'll see, being super-connected isn't just a way to extract value from your network. Creating new and valuable connections inside your existing network is a useful way to become a super-connector.

From Shy to Super-Connected

Like Brian Grazer's network, Jordan Harbinger's network rests on the upper limits of the power law. Like Grazer, Harbinger is a super-connector. Unlike Grazer, however, Harbinger didn't develop his network from a natural curiosity and desire to seek out interesting conversations. Rather, he built his abnormally large network out of necessity. Growing up, Jordan was a shy kid. He skipped school a lot because he experienced social anxiety whenever he was there. He wasn't a bad student—quite the opposite in fact. He was smart enough and hardworking enough to graduate from the University of Michigan and eventually go on to law school there as well.[18]

In law school, Harbinger realized just how important it was to build his network. It was during his internship that he learned that "what you know" wasn't as good a path to success as "who you know." And he learned that he ought to know a *lot* of people. During a summer internship, Harbinger was working at a Wall Street law firm, and by luck of the draw, he was paired with a "mentor" whom he could never seem to find. Apparently, his mentor was always out of the office (more on exactly why a little bit later). Harbinger looked around at the firm and saw a company built seemingly on hard work alone. "These guys, they bill in six-minute increments," Harbinger explained of the lawyers at the firm. "That'd be my job too. You want to bill as many hours as possible. Then a senior partner will decide what a reasonable amount of time is for you to do a specific task."[19]

From his perspective, it was all about putting in the work. "You bill 2,000-plus hours a year. You get a bonus. Life is grand," he said. "It's a lot of work, though."

That was when Harbinger finally met his assigned mentor, Dave. "He was never in the office," Harbinger recalled. "This was a guy from Brooklyn who had a tan . . . so obviously he knew something that nobody else knew."[20] Harbinger only got one meeting with Dave, and the only reason that meeting happened was that human resources, realizing that Dave hadn't met his mentee for that summer yet, made it happen.

"We were at Starbucks, and he's standing there and goes 'Well, ask me whatever you want,'" Harbinger recalled. Dave barely looked up from his BlackBerry as Harbinger started with the most obvious question: "How come you're never in the office?"[21] Harbinger had watched as other lawyers in the firm worked all hours of the day and even into the weekend. Yet Dave was never around and looked like he was earning the same money as a partner.

Dave decided to return the candor. "I bring in the deals," he said. "I bring in clients. I bring in customers. I've got the book of business."[22] Dave explained that he didn't bill for nearly as many hours as the other lawyers, but he made up for it in compensation with his referral bonuses. Dave saw his job less as working long hours in the office and more as working his contacts to generate new clients for the firm. So while others were working away to grow their tally of billable hours, Dave was working as a "rainmaker" to grow his tally of contacts and connections that might someday help the firm.

When they got back to the office, Harbinger started doing the math. His mentor wasn't putting in enough billable hours to make his bonus, but he was getting a percentage of the total legal bill for any clients he brought into the firm, which meant he was making more than most of the other partners. For Harbinger, a lightbulb went off; indeed, it was a turning point in his career strategy. As an undergraduate, he could see that intelligence brought a person pretty far. In law school, it seemed like intelligence and hard work were the right combination. But what he now saw was that in the outside world, even intelligence and hard work alone weren't enough. *He would need to start building his network.*

Harbinger returned for his final year at law school and immediately started putting what he had learned over the summer into practice. He wasn't just studying networking. He studied nonverbal communication, body language, vocal tonality, conversational dynamics, and a host of other topics that would help him grow his connections. He borrowed lessons from dating and relationships and took what worked into building professional relationships. He built a small-scale study group that led to huge demand among students to get to know Jordan because they realized it could help their academic performance.

Then he started teaching what he knew. Along with a fellow

graduate student from a different program, Harbinger started convening meetings and giving lessons to other people in how to build networks. In Ann Arbor, they had attracted a small but loyal following of people wanting to know more about how to succeed with relationships, both personal and professional. Eventually, they started looking for ways to scale. In 2006, Harbinger and his partner got an idea. "There was this new thing called podcasting, where you record a conversation and put it online and people can download it," he said.[23] With that, Harbinger started building an Internet radio show. They had to piece together equipment from music shops, as most microphones weren't set up to be plugged into a computer, but they made it work and were online shortly thereafter.

While they built a much larger audience just by taking their conversations online, the podcast also provided Harbinger with a new way to practice his skills in building and maintaining connections: he started looking for experts to come on the show as guests. In many cases, Harbinger simply had to reach out cold to individuals, build rapport quickly, and invite them on the show. But as the audience grew and his roster of past guests grew, he started to realize that making connections between people in his existing network was a much better way both to grow his contacts and to serve his community. "I was floating in these circles now, and yes, I would use the network to help me find the next guests," he said. "But I also didn't cut people off if they couldn't help me. In fact, if they weren't a good guest, my default strategy was to try and help them."[24] Whenever he met new people, he would map through his own network as he talked to them and try to find someone to connect them with who could help them.

"Every single person you meet has tremendous potential value to everybody else that you know," Harbinger said.[25] It's the secret he has been using for ten years to build a top-ranked podcast, *The Art of Charm,* which now has around 5 million monthly listeners. It's also the secret he's used to build his own network nearly as large.

Harbinger focuses on making valuable connections in and among contacts in his network, and in turn the network feeds him connections that would be valuable guests on his show. When he says every single person has value to someone else, he is using the language of a super-connector. And his life and career testify to the fact that anyone can become one. From a shy kid skipping school because of social anxiety, he became a business owner who (when asked) couldn't actually count the number of people in his network or his address book. Over ten years, Harbinger has risen to the top of the power law—and so have his show and the business he built around it.

While we may think our networks are only as powerful as our connections are themselves—like cards in a hand of poker—the research from network sciences offers a different truth. Some people play their hands better because they are holding the entire deck. These super-connectors have developed powerful connections by developing a lot of connections. The ability to become a super-connector isn't limited to a select few. With time and effort, anyone can become a super-connector, and as we'll see in the next chapter, it might even get easier the more you work at it.

FROM SCIENCE TO PRACTICE

As Jordan Harbinger learned, and as Brian Grazer's Hollywood career demonstrates, a big part of becoming a super-connector is serving the people in your network by connecting others. Being generous with introductions adds value to those around you, but it also makes it more likely that others will reciprocate and be generous in introducing you to their contacts. It's best if you can make introductions part of your regular routine, aiming for a goal of about one introduction or more per week. If you have never felt comfortable making introductions, here is a helpful format you can utilize in almost any situation, using any medium:

1. Start with a brief line introducing each person by name ("John, meet Jane; Jane, meet John").
2. Briefly cover the background of each person ("Jane is . . ."), with roughly a paragraph's worth of information per person.
3. Add a short comment about why you think these two people would benefit from connecting ("You both work in the same industry . . .").
4. End with a brief call to action, specifying what should happen next and who should initiate it ("John, would you be kind enough to jump on a phone call with Jane in the next week?").

Depending on the busyness of one party or the other, you can adapt this format to a "double opt-in" introduction. Here you reach out privately to each person first (using information from steps 2 and 3); once both people consent, your actual introduction will be even shorter (mostly just information from steps 1 and 4).

In addition, once introductions become part of your routine, you will regularly start thinking about your existing network when you meet new people. When making introductions has become almost second nature, you will be acting like a super-connector in your current network and be well on your way to growing a super-connector's network.

Practicing Online

While some social media services make introductions even easier, enabling you to link to people at the push of a button, it's best to stay away from these options. If you are not comfortable sending each person an email introduction, then your relationship to one or both of them probably isn't strong enough. If so, introducing them via social media is more likely to be seen as an annoyance than a benefit.

For a downloadable template to use when completing this exercise, go to http://davidburkus.com/resources/ and look for networking resources.

— 7 —

LEVERAGE PREFERENTIAL ATTACHMENT

Or
Why the Most Connected People Tend to Stay That Way

We tend to look at super-connectors, with their large-scale networks, and marvel at how much work it must take to build and maintain such a collection of contacts. But research reveals a surprising fact about connections: they get easier to make over time. The more connections you have, the more likely you are to make new connections. So building a valuable network might seem like a lot of work now, but eventually it will become effortless.

When the bank called Jayson Gaignard about his business loan, he didn't think much of it. They were calling in his loan and demanding that he pay in full immediately. It was a little bit of a problem, but not one he couldn't overcome. He had built the company on a substantial cash flow, so paying the bank wasn't much of a problem.

But what happened after that was.

Gaignard's business, Tickets Canada, had started as a concierge service for wealthy customers in the Toronto, Ontario, area. "If it was legal, moral, and it would save you time, we'd take care of it," Gaignard explained.[1] The service fielded a variety of different requests—some of them right up against that legal/moral line—but over time the majority of his customers started asking for help buying concert tickets in particular. This was a reasonable request since dinner reservations and tickets were standard add-ons when booking the services of a hotel concierge. When demand for concert tickets grew so high that Gaignard's company had become the second-largest ticket wholesaler in Canada, it rebranded itself as Tickets Canada.

The business was going well, drawing in around $6 million per year in revenue, but Gaignard wasn't happy. He didn't feel like the business was making much of an impact on the world, and preparing the business for sale would take another year of work to install the systems needed for someone to run the business without him at the center. And the bank calling in the loan didn't help that much either. But because of their cash flow, he was able to pay off the loan easily; they would just have to buy less inventory for a time and then work their way back.

Then Gaignard got another phone call. This call was from his merchant services provider. Because the majority of the business ran on credit card transactions, there was always a risk of charge-backs and disputed charges. Gaignard's company had historically low rates of charge-backs, especially for the tickets industry. Nonetheless, the merchant services company had decided that ticket businesses were high-risk and announced that, effective immediately, it would be keeping 100 percent of credit card revenues in its escrow for a full six months in case of charge-backs. With one phone call, Gaignard's cash flow had effectively slowed to a dribble. To stay in business, he started taking on debt once again. After taking on $250,000 in loans, and still waiting on their income to come out of escrow, his business was effectively done.

Gaignard needed a new plan. He had bet his last chips and lost, and even those in his own network started looking at him as bad luck. Eventually, no one was returning his calls. He had, as he counted it, zero people in his network. "I got married in 2012," Gaignard explained, "and the only two people who showed up at my bachelor party were my brother and my future brother-in-law."[2] Everyone had pretty much left him. He needed a way to start over, not just with a new business but with a new network.

"I was sitting in a workshop with Seth Godin in New York," Gaignard recalled. A friend had given him his spare ticket to the workshop. "And Godin told the story of a man named Thornton May. The gist of the story is that May was in business development for an IT firm and realized that CIOs were often disconnected from their peers. So Thornton started visiting different big cities and working to connect the CIOs via events, breakfasts, dinners, etc. Nothing in it for him at first, but as he became known as the host of these events, the CIOs started sending him business."[3] Gaignard wondered if a similar tactic might work for him—it might be a way to rebuild his network and to find his next business idea.

So he started planning dinners. His idea was quite simple. Gaignard felt that entrepreneurs were some of the loneliest people in business. Not lonely because they had no one to interact with, but lonely because they rarely had the chance to interact with other entrepreneurs. He would start hosting dinners to change all of that. Of course, there was one problem. He didn't really have much of a network with entrepreneurs. He had been so busy building his tickets business that he had let relationships fall by the wayside.

Without a community of entrepreneurs already built, Gaignard had to find one. Fortunately, he had a pretty good list to pick from. Every year in Canada, *Canadian Business* magazine publishes its Profit 500 list—the top 500 fastest-growing companies in Canada. Gaignard simply cold-called the entrepreneurs on that list who lived near him and made his pitch. "I'm doing a dinner for the Profit list alumni. If you're interested, let me know," Gaignard would say. He lost count of how many cold calls he made, but he got eight commitments for his first dinner.

As quickly as he had momentum, however, Gaignard almost lost it. His nerves started to get the better of him. "I almost canceled two hours prior. I was so worried that no one would see the value in it and would think I'd wasted their time," he recalled. He worried about being twice labeled a failure. But just the opposite happened. The evening was a huge success. From the moment his guests arrived, the conversations didn't skip a beat. Gaignard had created a cluster of entrepreneurs who immediately recognized the value of having a small insider group in which to share challenges and advice—even if they all came from different businesses in different industries. "We had people from tech, we had another who had a moving business, another guy in the office furniture business," Gaignard said. "And I knew from this one dinner that connecting entrepreneurs—connecting people—was something that energized me and that I could spend my life doing."[4]

After a few more dinners and a few more successes, word about Gaignard's "Mastermind Dinners" began to spread. Demand began to grow. And so did his network. Former guests would refer new guests, and Gaignard also kept cold-calling new potential guests. But he was looking for a way to scale it faster—not just his own network but the whole network of entrepreneurs he was building.

Also, keeping everything together was getting costly. Gaignard was picking up the tab for these dinners, he was still carrying his debt from his last businesses, and new money wasn't coming in. "My wife, my daughter, and I were basically living off of American Express gift cards," Gaignard said. But to him it was worth it. "I kept thinking that the bank can take my car, they can take whatever assets I have, but they can't take my relationships."[5] Eventually, Gaignard figured, those relationships would turn up a revenue opportunity. Little did he know that the relationships would turn *into* the revenue opportunity.

After a successful run of Mastermind Dinners, Jayson stumbled upon a unique opportunity. A best-selling business author who rarely spoke in public was offering to speak at any event provided that the event planners purchased 4,000 copies of his newest book. The author was in a hurry, however, and wanted to do the deal right away; in effect, it was first-come-first-served. At first, Gaignard thought of a friend in his newly formed network of entrepreneurs who would be interested. However, he worried that by the time he got a hold of that friend someone else would have claimed the offer. So Gaignard emailed the author quickly and claimed the package for himself. Now he just needed to find $84,000 to purchase 4,000 books.

Thinking through his network, he thought of three new connections who would be interested in helping him plan an event and make a return off of the book investment. The first turned Gaignard down after he couldn't provide any estimates or projections (the business idea was only a few hours old). The second person was interested in the idea, but only as a first step in a larger business (but Gaignard didn't know where any of this would lead). The third contact was the charm. He listened intently to Gaignard's pitch, then responded, "Swing by my office tomorrow to pick up a check." He would loan Gaignard the money, but with no contract, no repayment terms, just a handshake agreement.

With the money, and eventually the books, Gaignard expanded on his Mastermind Dinners concept and created an event he labeled "Mastermind Talks." The idea was simple. Just as the dinners brought together about a dozen entrepreneurs to make connections and talk shop, his event would bring together 100 entrepreneurs for the same level of connection-building and experience-sharing. And just like the dinners, the event was a huge success. Not only did it strengthen the network of entrepreneurs in the community, but planning and executing the event dramatically increased Gaignard's network as well.

Since that first day, Gaignard has made Mastermind Talks an annual event. The event is capped at 150 entrepreneurs, and from one year to the next, only around 75 to 80 people are allowed to return—the rest are encouraged to rotate off to allow new people to enter the community. That rotation accelerated the process of building Gaignard's network even more. "The majority of our new attendees come from the referrals of previous attendees," Gaignard said.[6] So with each entrepreneur who attends, Gaignard's network expands two- to threefold as attendees recommend new people.

Jayson Gaignard wasn't always a super-connector. In fact, he dislikes the term. But today he has a super-connector's network. His contact list numbers in the tens of thousands—a significant increase from having only two people at his bachelor party. As Mastermind Talks continues, Gaignard's network grows itself. Instead of actively seeking to add new connections, he now sees his role as pruning and strengthening to enhance the quality of his relationships inside of the Mastermind Talks community, not just adding to the quantity of it. "When I started out, the second time, it was me pushing hard for the first few years. I was joining other communities, going to networking events, doing everything I could to try and meet people," Gaignard said. "Now we're at the point where demand for Mastermind Talks, referrals of new attendees from previous guests, means my network grows exponentially and organically. So my focus now is more the pruning of it and going deep with certain individuals to build the best community around me."[7]

Gaignard became so focused on community and connections because his path to becoming super-connected taught him the importance of relationships. After the first event, Gaignard was quickly able to repay his $84,000 handshake loan. When he did, he asked his lender a question: "I was a quarter of a million dollars in debt. I was the worst investment you could ever make. Why'd you do it?" The entrepreneur's reply was simple. He wasn't investing in the business idea. He was investing in Gaignard. "At that point, two things became clear. One is that you never know the value of your network until you need it. And two is that when you hit rock bottom, you'll be left with only two things: your word and your relationships."[8]

Beyond the importance of these two factors, Gaignard's experience also outlines a surprising truth about connections and communities. While we might look at people with large-scale networks and marvel at how much work it must take to build and maintain such a large network, the truth is that it gets easier over time. As your network grows, as the number of your connections increases, the process of meeting new people becomes easier. Not because you get more practiced at making introductions, but because introductions are more likely to find you. It's a phenomenon that network scientists call *preferential attachment,* and it explains why the most connected are most likely to stay that way, but also why building your network will take less and less work over time.

The Rich Get Richer, and the Connected Get More Connected

That there is a connection between how many contacts you have and how likely you are to meet new people shouldn't surprise anyone. We have been using phrases like "the rich get richer" for some time now to discuss how initial advantages beget more advantages. In sociology, there is even a term for it: the *Matthew effect*. The term comes from a puzzling passage in the Bible, in the Gospel of Matthew, where Jesus says: "For to all those who have, more will be given, and they will have an abundance; but from those who have nothing, even what they have will be taken away."[9]

Sociologists have picked up on this theme as well. In fact, this biblical saying was initially applied by the sociologist Robert Merton to fame, social status, and eventually capital.[10] But in studying social network relationships, Barabási and Albert found that the Matthew effect applies to making new contacts as well.

Recall from the previous chapter that Barabási and Albert were studying the emergence of power laws in networks. They had noticed that, in many networks, the number of connections an individual node (or person) has varies wildly. Instead of there being a well-defined average with only minor deviation, networks tend to follow a power law, they discovered, whereby a few nodes hold massive numbers of connections and the count declines rapidly.

Having found these power laws, Barabási and Albert wanted to know why they occurred. What was it about the mysterious nature of networks that allowed for the more connected ("the rich") to grow even more connected? It's hard to see in hindsight, but discovering the presence of power laws in network science had been a disruption of the norm. Before Barabási and Albert's work, most models of networks assigned to a fixed number of nodes connections made at random — or seemingly at random.

In trying to find an explanation for power laws, Barabási and Albert introduced two new concepts to the realm of network science.[11] The first was growth. Most models of networks were static, fixed in time and never changing. But real-world networks, particularly networks of humans, evolve. They change often, and the most common change is the entry of new people into a network. Over time networks have to grow — and new people have to connect somewhere.

The second concept was what they labeled *preferential attachment*. If growth is assumed, and if growth always means that new people have to connect somewhere, then given a choice between two nodes with which to connect, new nodes are more likely to connect to the more-connected node. If a node is twice as connected as another, then it should also be twice as likely to make a connection to new nodes. When new people enter a network, preferential attachment assumes that they are more likely to meet highly connected individuals than those off on the fringes.

Think about your own experiences. Not only do super-connectors tend to offer the most potential introductions to others in the network, but others in the network are more likely to introduce you to other people who are already super-connectors. Enter a new community and pick any random person; if that person is already more likely to be connected to the well connected, then eventually you will be too. Barabási and Albert saw this as a real-world phenomenon and argued that any realistic model of networks needed to take preferential attachment into account.

Having made their propositions about network growth and preferential attachment, Barabási and Albert next had to provide proof. To do this, they wanted to use well-known, well-respected data sets.[12] If you guessed that they chose the network of film actors from the "six degrees of Kevin Bacon" study, you're right. They also examined the network of scientific citations and the world wide web (a massive and ever-evolving network).

At first blush, a network of websites linking to other websites might seem like an odd focus of study. After all, what implications can we draw from computers that link to other computers? But Barabási and Albert were studying the world wide web in the late 1990s, a time when the majority of links and connections between websites were still made manually—by humans—and as such would be representative of a human network. In each situation, preferential attachment held true. As new nodes entered the network, they were more likely to connect to the already well connected. As a result, small initial differences in the number of connections held by an actor, scientist, or website increased as the network grew. "Preferential attachment induces a rich-get-richer phenomenon that helps the more connected nodes grab a disproportionately large number of links at the expense of the latecomers," Barabási explained.[13]

Shortly after Barabási and Albert published their results in the prestigious journal *Science,* Mark Newman, a professor of physics at the University of Michigan and faculty member of the Santa Fe Institute, examined the influence of preferential attachment on a grander scale.[14] Newman collected six years of publication data from two large databases of scientific research, one in physics and one in biology and medicine. Taken together, they represented around 1.7 million people. He used that data to construct two large-scale network models (one for physics and one for biology/medicine). In particular, he looked at the number of scientists' previous collaborations and the number of collaborators they'd had. Sure enough, he found strong evidence of preferential attachment. Those with a high number of previous collaborators were more likely to enter into new collaborations. And this preferential attachment was indeed the most likely source of the power law seen when graphing the number of connections. In other words, *the more connected were becoming even more connected because when new people enter a network, they are more likely to connect with those who are already highly connected.*

Interestingly, preferential attachment appears to affect more than just individuals' connections. A similar phenomenon can be seen in the way individuals develop preferences and tastes and in how they make decisions. What is already popular seems to grow even more so when new people enter the system and have to decide what to prefer—as robustly demonstrated in a study conducted by Matthew Salganik, Peter Dodds, and Duncan Watts.[15] The trio designed an experiment to investigate how preferences grow and compound over time and whether a phenomenon like preferential attachment applies to popularity as well. To do this, they first built a website where participants could log in, listen to forty-eight different songs, and then download them for free. More than 14,000 people logged in to the site. But in actuality, 14,000-plus people logged in to one of nine "worlds" that appeared to be mirror images of each other. In the first world, users would log in and see a list with the name of the song and the band or artist. (All of the options, it's worth noting, were unknown songs performed by unknown bands.) In the other eight worlds, users would see the same information, plus how many times previous users had downloaded the song.

In setting up these different worlds, Salganik and his colleagues were able to observe whether initial differences in downloads affected the overall popularity of songs by the time the experiment concluded. Theoretically, if the quality of a song alone determined its popularity, then all eight worlds where the download count was available to users should have roughly matched the one world where download count wasn't displayed. Better-quality songs should have been more popular, and lesser-quality ones less so. Except that's not what happened.

Despite all of the songs starting at zero, later users took their cue from early users who had listened to and downloaded songs and were more likely to sample those songs too. Small differences in popularity turned into big differences over time, and the songs that benefited from that small difference also varied between worlds. In one world, one song in particular was number one by the end of the experiment, but in a different world it was fortieth out of the forty-eight. In every world, the most downloaded song early on became even more downloaded. The rich got even richer.

Just as we are more likely to be introduced to, or seek out introductions to, already well-connected individuals, we are more likely to take cues from those around us about what to listen to or what to like. These findings call into question a lot of what we know about breakout hit songs, blockbuster movies, best-selling books, and famous celebrities. The quality of the given work or performance may not be all that affects its acclaim. Instead, its growing popularity might be simply a result of who you know—or more specifically, how many friends and friends of friends you know—who already enjoy that work. Salganik and his colleagues demonstrated this clearly inside the lab. But a close look at history reveals that we are likely more affected by preferential attachment and social influence than we know.

The Most Famous Smile in the World . . . Because It's the Most Famous Smile in the World

The most famous female face in the world is arguably that of Lisa Gherardini.[16] Her husband was a wealthy silk merchant who had commissioned a portrait of his wife. The portrait took some time, and neither Gherardini nor her husband ever saw the finished product. Hopefully, they never had to pay for it either. When it was finally finished, sixteen years after it was commissioned, it was sold to France's King François I. The seller was the Italian artist and inventor Leonardo da Vinci, and the painting was the *Mona Lisa*. It is now perhaps the most famous painting in the world, though a few others by Leonardo himself might rival its fame. It hangs in Paris's Musée du Louvre behind a climate-controlled, entirely bulletproof case. Six million people visit the painting in person every year. Hundreds of millions more see reproductions of it on everything from posters to coffee cups, tote bags, and T-shirts. It has been photographed, parodied, forged, and far worse (as we'll see).

But perhaps the most curious thing about the painting wasn't how long it took Leonardo to finish it, but how long it took to become famous. Though it was completed in 1519, it spent its first 300 years as little more than a hallway decoration for European royalty. It wasn't considered terrible—just ordinary. When it was eventually moved to the Louvre around the turn of the nineteenth century, it didn't garner much attention: Leonardo wasn't really considered a spectacular painter until the mid-1800s. And the *Mona Lisa* likely would have remained hanging in obscurity in the halls of the Louvre, appreciated only by art critics and historians, had it not been for an audacious act of patriotism—and theft.

On August 21, 1911, a group of men led by Vincenzo Peruggia stole the *Mona Lisa*.[17] Peruggia was Italian, and some accounts say he was upset that a painting by the Italian legend Leonardo was stuck in a French museum.[18] The four men snuck into the museum the night before; Peruggia arranged for their entry, as he was working on the museum's renovation at the time.[19] They spent the night sleeping hidden in a storeroom. The following morning, a national holiday, they awoke, seized the painting off the wall, and hurried out a side entrance. No one saw them, and if they had, they would have assumed they were merely workmen. No one noticed that the painting was gone until twenty-six hours later—partly because of the holiday and partly because the painting was not very popular.

Then something funny happened. Peruggia and his crew had indeed stolen an unpopular painting—but the theft of the *Mona Lisa* propelled it to extreme popularity. Within forty-eight hours, news of the theft had spread around the world. People began hanging wanted posters around Paris and crowds gathered at police stations. Rumors and conspiracy theories sprang up. Some argued that the whole thing was a hoax. Others claimed it was the work of an international ring of art thieves and black-market collectors. In a desperate attempt to chase down every lead, police even interrogated Pablo Picasso, one of many painters they assumed might know how to track down the painting's whereabouts. To their credit, they also interrogated Peruggia himself. However, he was able to talk his way out of it, claiming that, on the morning in question, he was hungover from the night before.

All the while, the painting sat hidden under a false bottom in a wooden trunk inside of Peruggia's room in a Parisian boardinghouse. It would stay there for two years until Peruggia eventually took a train to Florence, Italy, in order to meet with an art dealer who would find a way to sell the painting and have it displayed in the famous Uffizi Gallery.[20] But after meeting Peruggia in his hotel room to view the painting, the art dealer promptly called the police.

Peruggia was arrested, and the painting was eventually returned to the Louvre. It was visited by more than 100,000 people in the first two days of being returned to display.[21] Within a few years, the painting began to draw the attention of prominent artists of the era. In 1919, the French painter Marcel Duchamp created a parody of the painting, adding a goatee and mustache —along with a crude caption.[22] Spanish painter Salvador Dalí created a portrait of himself as the *Mona Lisa,* complete with a mustache similar to Duchamp's. American artist Andy Warhol chose the *Mona Lisa* as an influence for many works using his silk-screen technique. Since then, the painting has been parodied hundreds of times, including the *Mona Lisa* with a unibrow, the *Mona Lisa* as an astronaut, the *Mona Lisa* as Batman, and even the *Mona Lisa* as a LEGO mini-figure. It has also been a target of more crime—not theft but, on two occasions, vandalism. Despite the parodies, attacks, and inspired replications, the *Mona Lisa*'s popularity only seems to rise.

While today's art critics and historians debate the merits of the painting—what with its exceptional demonstration of Leonardo's technique and his influential role in Renaissance painting—it cannot be forgotten or ignored how uninfluential the painting was until Peruggia's theft. Instead, just as with preferential attachment, the painting lay in obscurity for hundreds of years before an inciting event skyrocketed it into popularity. And with every successive generation, new people are introduced to the *Mona Lisa* as the world's most famous painting—like new participants viewing the download counts of songs in Salganik's experiment, or new entrants into a network being told they "have to meet" the already well-connected members.

Preferential attachment influences our decisions more than most of us realize. And that is both bad news and good news. The bad news is that building a network, or building awareness for your new brand, product, or company, is an uphill battle. The good news is that it gets easier over time. In addition, as the next chapter will uncover, it's possible to leverage preferential attachment inside even a small-scale network to become (or at least appear) extremely well connected. The scientific evidence and examples as diverse as entrepreneurship networks and famous art suggest that eventually that hill is crested and the journey gets easier. It might take a lot of initial hustle, but that hustle can slow down as early investments in building relationships begin to pay dividends by bringing relationships to you.

FROM SCIENCE TO PRACTICE

As Jayson Gaignard learned, dinners and other large events can be a great way to scale your network of contacts faster. Unlike grabbing a quick coffee with just one or two people, sharing a meal allows you to connect to a dozen or more people at once for several hours, building more and deeper connections. In addition, depending on the structure of the dinner, it can be a way to leverage preferential attachment no matter how small your network is.

You can host dinners (or lunches) in your own city or your own home, or you can regularly plan to host a dinner when you are traveling to connect with old contacts (and make new ones) in each city you visit. To make sure your event is a success, there are a few things you have to consider:

1. *The size:* At a minimum, invite six people. A gathering any smaller than that can make new people feel left out as old friends reconnect. At a maximum, make it no more than twelve people. Any more than that and not everyone will get a chance to interact with every other guest.
2. *The guests:* Ideally, you want a good mix of old friends and new contacts. You can do that by reaching out cold to people you want to invite or asking for an introduction through a friend. If you don't know such a person, then ask your guests to bring a plus-one — not in the romantic sense but a person that the entire group would benefit from knowing.
3. *The location:* Your home is a great choice, as it's personal and comfortable enough to encourage people to linger. If you are traveling or need to host the event in a restaurant, make sure you coordinate with the manager ahead of time to en-

sure that you get a large table in a quiet area (and to make sure everyone is clear on how the bill will be settled).

4. *The frequency:* If it's your first event ever, don't worry so much about this one. However, once you try it and it works, you need to think about how frequently (weekly, twice a month, monthly, quarterly) you would like to hold events. Just one time is not enough to leverage preferential attachment.

Practicing Online

If you are traveling to another city and decide to host an event, your existing social media presence can be a big help. Most social network services allow you to search for connections by city, and the ease of communication can make it a great medium to plan an event. Manage invitations this way, and even start meeting new invitees.

For a downloadable template to use when completing this exercise, go to http://davidburkus.com/resources/ and look for networking resources.

— 8 —

CREATE THE ILLUSION OF MAJORITY

Or
Why No One Is as Popular as They Seem

If we want to be known within a community of people, we often think we need to meet every single person in it or use an outreach medium that gets everyone in touch all at once. However, research into social networks reveals that it's the most connected individuals who tend to guide the perceptions of the overall group. This means that we can have the appearance of being everywhere and in demand — by only focusing on a few of the right connections.

BEFORE WRITING HIS FIRST BOOK, Tim Ferriss was basically a vitamin salesman. Granted, he was also a kickboxing champion, a world record–holding tango dancer, an investor, and an adviser to big-name start-up companies. But he himself wasn't a big name. Ferriss had started an online company marketing a vitamin formula designed to enhance brain function that was aimed at athletes. He had adjusted the business to run mostly on autopilot and chronicled his process in a book he titled "Drug Dealing for Fun and Profit."[1] On the advice of his publisher, the title was changed to *The Four-Hour Workweek*. Now Ferriss had a real challenge. He was new to bookselling, so none of his past success would be any help to him in marketing this new product.

But Ferriss had a plan for achieving optimal results from minimum effort there as well. He knew his target group specifically. "18–35 [-year-old] tech-savvy males," he recalled. "Partially because I'm in that demographic."[2] And because he was in that group, he also knew that he didn't need to spend time getting the attention of the big media players that most newbie authors salivate after. He didn't need the *New York Times* to review his book, or to land an interview on *Good Morning America*. Instead, he went small. "I identified the primary channels through which I could achieve a surround sound effect," he explained. "I identified that there were, let's just say, 10 to 15 blogs and if I hit 50 percent of those on any given week, I would create the perception, and to some extent, the reality, that I was ubiquitous."[3] He believed he could make eighteen- to thirty-five-year-old tech-savvy males notice him as often as if he had chased down every possible publicity stunt, but without really doing so.

So Ferriss identified his precise targets, the ten to fifteen most popular niche websites in that demographic, and focused on developing relationships with them. He would go to conferences, meet writers from those publications for drinks, and ask them lots of questions about themselves and their work. "I never played the 'I know what's perfect for your audience' card, ever," he said. But eventually these reporters would ask Ferriss what he was working on. He would tell them he was working on a book and then give them a little about what it was about, then offer to send them a copy. "That was it," he recalled. "That was the business plan."[4]

It worked. Most of the journalists ended up writing about Ferriss or about an idea in his book, and most of them did it at the same time. Ferriss had created a media illusion among those eighteen- to thirty-five-year-old tech-savvy males that he was being talked about everywhere. Eventually, word began to spread. His book became a bestseller, which led to more publicity, which actually did lead to it being talked about in the *New York Times* and his being interviewed on *Good Morning America*. Ferriss had made himself look like he was everywhere without actually having to be almost anywhere.

And he is not the only one. Entrepreneur Andrew Davis used a similar strategy to launch not one but two businesses and grow them exponentially in a short period of time.

No matter where you begin, Davis started his career originally in television, either as a childhood commercial actor or as a producer and writer for the Jim Henson Company later on as an adult. But he quickly pivoted to working with Internet start-ups. "It was the first dot-com boom in 1998 and 1999," he recalled. "All my friends who were in television were leaving to work in marketing, and they were making four times as much as me. It felt like everybody I knew."[5]

So Davis left television and joined a start-up. "That's where I learned how to apply all these things from television to marketing," he said. He also learned quickly that many marketers were doing it poorly. As a result, it wasn't long before he went out on his own. In 2001, he started a marketing agency called Tippingpoint Labs. They had great ideas about storytelling and content marketing, but they needed clients. Like a lot of agencies starting out, Davis and Tippingpoint would take whatever work came in the door and were simply working to grow the company. But after several years of this kind of haphazard growth, they felt something was off. "We decided we needed to get much more focused, because we were hiring more people and we were doing disparate work for people who we didn't really love," Davis said. "So we decided to take a much more strategic approach to growth and in growing the business."[6]

That strategic approach came in the form of selecting specific industries and speaking just to them. Literally speaking to them at their conferences and events. Davis had already seen that speaking at conferences could be a useful tool for gaining more clients, but Tippingpoint's scattershot approach had kept them running from niche to niche and never really establishing a foothold as the go-to agency for anyone.

The first industry they chose was construction and housing. "This was 2009; the housing market had kind of imploded," said Davis, but therein lay the opportunity. "They were struggling to figure out what they were going to do from a marketing standpoint, and we thought it was a great opportunity for us to stand out."[7]

So Davis looked up the biggest trade publisher in the construction space and reached out to the editor in chief of their different magazines. He then gave him his pitch: "Look, I know you have your annual event coming up, and I know the budgets are tight. I'd love to speak at your annual event. I speak a lot, but I've never spoken in this vertical, so to lower your risk you can just pay my travel."[8] This approach worked: Davis got the invitation to keynote the event. He was going to give the closing address of a three-day conference—the climax of the event.

To get up to speed, he showed up at the conference on the very first day. "I would basically sit in the audience of every session I could possibly attend for two days," he laughed. "I'd learn as much as I could about the industry; I'd learn all the acronyms and vernacular of the industry. Then I'd take my normal domain expertise in marketing and apply it to their market."[9] It paid off. Davis's talk was well received, and afterwards he was flooded with prospective clients . . . and invitations to speak at other industry events.

Davis even found that his strategy was working for more than just events. "If you speak at a publisher's event, they invariably write about you on their website and in their magazine," he explained. "And they distribute the videos and all of the sudden, even people who weren't at the event start either inviting you to speak or are aware of the service you provide or of your expertise in the market."[10] Like Tim Ferriss with tech-savvy males, Davis's small actions in targeting the major voices in an industry had turned him quickly into the hot topic.

And Tippingpoint Labs didn't stop there. The next year they repeated the formula, but this time did so in financial services. Then the following year they targeted fast food and quick service restaurants. Then travel and tourism. Each year they extended their expertise into a new vertical and quickly became the most talked-about option. And each time they did this by targeting the biggest, most connected trade publisher in the space and appearing at its event, then letting speaking invitations and referrals push them easily into the lead.

By 2012, Davis was spending most of his time during the workweek traveling to events in these different verticals and generating new leads for the agency. That was when he pivoted again and started a new business. Davis sold his interest back to the agency, wrote a book on branding and marketing, and started out on his own with a company of one. One at a time, Davis started revisiting the same contacts he had first made at trade magazines and pitched his speaking. "I basically said, 'I have a book and I already know your industry, and you know me well; you've seen me speak,'" Davis said. "'Except I'm not free anymore.'"[11]

To his pleasant surprise, the strategy worked. More and more referrals for speaking started coming in, and it was largely because people were spreading the word in between events about this new expert they were hearing from. Sometimes he would hear from prospective clients inviting him to speak, and they would say he was recommended by three different people. "They're like, 'Wow, I just heard about this guy yesterday from another person. I've never even heard of this person, but now everybody's telling me they're reading this book,'" Davis said.[12]

Like Tim Ferriss, Andrew Davis has had an experience that's a testament to a weird phenomenon: appearing to be everywhere without actually being everywhere. Even if you're not selling a book, or a speech, or a long-term marketing contract, Ferriss's and Davis's experiences suggest that you can create the impression with an individual or a group that you are much better connected or better known than you really are. And the research into social networks seems to support this. The truth is, we routinely make judgments about other people, products, or trends based on what the social networks around us appear to be supporting.

But it is also possible that those same networks are tricking us into judging something as more popular than it is. It works a bit like an optical illusion; in fact, researchers refer to it as the *majority illusion*.

When Majorities Aren't

To understand how the majority illusion works, we first need to revisit a concept we have already covered: *super-connectors*. Recall that super-connectors are people on the highest point of a power law in terms of connections. The number of people in their network dramatically exceeds the number in the average person's network. Most people have a relatively small number of connections, and only a few people (such as super-connectors) have huge numbers of friends. In addition to super-connectors perhaps making you feel like you have a small network compared to theirs, the very existence of super-connectors skews the averages and makes almost everyone feel like they have a smaller network than their peers. The reason is quite simple: their network *is* smaller than average. In a network, most people have fewer friends or business contacts than the average.

This phenomenon is what those who study networks refer to as the *friendship paradox*. First asserted by Scott Feld, a sociologist at Purdue University, in his paper "Why Your Friends Have More Friends Than You Do," the friendship paradox stems from a contradiction to our optimism (or narcissism).[13] When surveyed, most people believe that they have *more* friends than their friends do. But when you sample a community or a cluster inside a social network, you find that most people have fewer friends than the average.

To better explain the paradox, consider an analogy to height. If you are a male and you measure the height of all of your male friends, you will find that the average is about 5 feet 9½ inches. If you plot the heights of all your friends on a graph, you will find this 5 feet 9½ inches to be pretty much the center, with a fairly even distribution on either side (the bell curve or inverted U shape we have discussed before). But now suppose that one of your friends is a lot taller than you. Not just a foot taller, but closer to 100 feet taller than you. This one person's height would dramatically skew the average. His height would ruin the average, pushing it much higher than 5 feet 9½ inches. Thus, you could confidently say that, *on average,* your friends are a lot taller than you—your hypothetical giant friend skews the average to guarantee it.

This is what is happening in social networks. Because a small group of people are capable of maintaining an especially large number of contacts, when you look across your network, you will find that, on average, your connections have more connections than you do. You might still have more connections than most, but the presence of those connectional giants will make your network appear smaller than average.

This dilemma became even worse with the invention of social media. The researchers Naghmeh Momeni and Michael Rabbit, both of McGill University, studied millions of Twitter users and hundreds of millions of tweets.[14] They found that the same power law applies inside online social networks. A small band of elite Twitter users have millions of followers; everyone else has far fewer. Thus, these Twitter "millionaires" skew the average enough that we can confidently say that the average Twitter user that you follow has more followers than you do (unless you happen to have 155,657 followers).

The presence of super-connectors (and the fact that connections follow a power law instead of a normal distribution) skews our perception of the network around us. But as Tim Ferriss and Andrew Davis learned, it is possible to play to this skew and appear more popular or more in demand than you really are.

This possibility was first proven only recently, by researchers at the University of Southern California led by Kristina Lerman.[15] Lerman and her colleagues were playing around with the friendship paradox and its connection to the idea that since we as humans can't see what our entire network is up to, we have to process interactions as they come and assess what the entire group is doing based on those people we interact with. Given this, it stands to reason that well-connected members of our network might skew our perception of how popular an idea or person actually is.

To test this, the researchers first created a model. The model showed a small-scale network of just fourteen people, with connections between people determined randomly. But what wasn't random was how many connections each person had. In the model, they were deliberately made to vary wildly—from just two connections to half the network. They then chose three people inside the model to be "active"—their term for any attribute to be represented, such as having red hair, owning an iPhone, or recommending Andrew Davis to speak.

When they chose the lowest-connected members of the network to be active, the number of people connected to other active persons through those connections was low . . . less than half of the total population. But when they chose the three highest-connected members, it was pretty easy to give off the appearance of popularity—everyone was connected to at least one active person, most were connected to two, and a few were even connected to all three active people. If you are sitting in this model and trying to judge the popularity of an idea, it is highly likely that you are hearing multiple people talk about it. Which can make it look like everyone is talking about it—even if only three people really are. Like tech blogs and Tim Ferriss, suddenly a minority of voices become the loudest sounds echoing throughout an entire network.

Having shown the phenomenon in small models, the researchers then increased the scale. Using computer simulations, the researchers built models as big as 10,000 people, all with varying degrees of connectedness. Not only did the majority illusion hold true, but in some models it was enhanced by bigger networks (since bigger networks meant a greater degree of variance when it came to the number of connections that each person had).

Building models inside a computer was one thing, but testing it in the real world was another. The researchers needed to know that the same phenomenon held true when the network scaled from 14 people to 14,000 or to 14 million. To do these tests, they collected data from three readily available networks. The first was the network of coauthorship of academic papers among high-energy physicists (which, as we've seen, is a great source of network data reflecting connections and collaborations). The second was the follower network of the social news aggregator Digg.com, and the third was the network of links among political blogs.

Among all three networks, they studied only mutual connections. In each case, the majority illusion held. Perhaps the most drastic example was in the world of political writing. "The effect is largest in the political blogs network," they wrote. "As many as 60%–70% of nodes will have a majority of active neighbors, even when only 20% of the nodes are active."[16] Just 20 percent of the political blogs could put forth an idea and the perception of any given node in the network would be that the majority of the network shared that belief. In other words, *the majority illusion explains how easy it is to trick a population into believing something is true and widely believed, when the reality is just the opposite.*

Just like the friendship paradox, the majority illusion happens because of the vast range of connections between different people in a network. Those with a lower number of connections, observing their more-connected colleagues put forth an idea or trend, conclude that the idea must be more popular than it really is. This can lead them to feel peer pressure (even though it's not a majority of their peers), and the idea or trend gets adopted even further. The majority illusion can become a self-fulfilling prophecy. And while we've seen how individuals like Tim Ferriss and Andrew Davis used it to create a self-fulfilling illusion of popularity, it turns out that whole companies have used the majority illusion, albeit unknowingly, to rapidly scale their business.

It's appropriate that perhaps the most drastic example of the majority illusion comes from the world's largest online social network—Facebook.

The World's Largest Small Community

Facebook wasn't supposed to become the world's largest online community, at least not at first. At first, it was just another dorm room side project of Harvard undergraduate Mark Zuckerberg and a few of his friends. Zuckerberg arrived on Harvard's campus in Cambridge, Massachusetts, in September 2003 and quickly got to work turning intriguing ideas into software and websites.[17] Within the first week, Zuckerberg had built a program called "Course Match." The idea behind it was to give his fellow students a fun way to pick classes based on who else was taking them. Students could click on a course to see the entire list of who had signed up or click on a specific person to see what other courses he or she was enrolled in. Did you want to know what other courses that cute girl in American History was taking? No problem: Course Match could tell you. It was a program that worked particularly well for the status-aware students of Harvard, who judged classes not on the content or the professors, but on who else in the community was enrolled. Almost immediately, hundreds of students had started using Course Match. The program was a hit. Zuckerberg's next project, however, wouldn't go over so well.

For his encore performance, Zuckerberg started a project he called Facemash. At the time, for each of its dormitories, Harvard had online "facebooks"—most of them no better in quality than a middle school yearbook—featuring student photos to make it easier for students to get to know each other. Zuckerberg decided to use these photos to present a more pressing question, especially among eighteen- and nineteen-year-old college students: who was the hottest person on campus? To do this, Zuckerberg created a computer program similar to how the worldwide ranking of chess players was determined—that is, each time one player played another one, the result affected the rankings—to rank the photos in as many online facebooks as he could find. The security and privacy for each dormitory facebook varied. With some of them, the photos were publicly available, with others he hacked into the website remotely, and with others he sneaked into the dormitories in order to use the private network and access the photos.

Within just eight hours, Zuckerberg had built a website that would put photos of two same-gender students next to each other and allow users to click on which one they felt was more attractive. As students were chosen, they moved up in the rankings and the program would compare them to other, hotter students. While the website instantly became popular, it didn't go over very well with the whole community. After significant backlash that all but ruined his on-campus reputation, Zuckerberg pulled the plug and moved on to a new project. This one would raise his reputation to heights he had never imagined.

Inspired by the popularity of emerging "social network websites" like Friendster and MySpace, and also "inspired," as some would say, by a project he was hired to work on by Cameron and Tyler Winklevoss, Zuckerberg and a collection of friends started a new kind of online social network. In January 2004, Zuckerberg registered the web address Thefacebook.com and started building. He and his friends had combined elements of Course Match and Facemash to create a service that invited individuals to create profiles of themselves, including personal information like hobbies, interests, and even romantic intentions. The service also featured a way to directly invite your friends via email to join as well. On February 4, 2004, the website was live and waiting to be discovered. They initially opened it up to only the Harvard community; an account could be created only with a Harvard .edu email address. Within Harvard, the service spread exponentially. By the end of February, 10,000 Harvard users had created a profile.[18] And no wonder.

As users joined the site, the service subtly encouraged them to email their friends and to invite them to join too, but only their Harvard friends. It didn't take long for non-users to see their email inbox flooded with invitations, or at least appear to be flooded with invitations. As the majority illusion would predict, as soon as a few highly connected individuals had profiles on Thefacebook, it would suddenly appear as though everyone at Harvard was online—and that they should be too.

Even if the majority illusion could easily explain it, the viral growth in popularity took even Zuckerberg by surprise. "Early on, we weren't intending this to be a company," Zuckerberg recalled. "We had no cash to run it."[19] But that initial and astounding success signaled something promising, and by the end of February they decided to expand beyond Harvard.

Unlike a lot of similar websites, Thefacebook didn't just open its doors to all comers. Where Friendster and MySpace were open to just about everyone who wanted to join, Zuckerberg and his team decided to expand in a relatively slow and controlled way, limiting who could join to college students at select universities. After Harvard had been dominated so easily, Thefacebook then opened up to Columbia, Yale, and Stanford by the end of February 2004. This deliberate one-college-at-a-time strategy was intended partly to resolve privacy concerns and partly to try to keep growth controlled. But as the majority illusion suggests, it might also have been the reason for Thefacebook's amazing early growth. Within a week of February 26, the day the site was opened to students at Stanford, more than half of the undergraduate population had signed up.

While it wasn't their intention, and they likely weren't even aware of it, the majority illusion was at work in Thefacebook, fueling its growth because of this campus-by-campus strategy. Rival online social networking websites like Friendster and MySpace, which were basically open from the beginning, worked pretty much the same on the surface. You would get an email invitation from someone you knew, you might or might not click on the email to visit the website and create an account, and then you would sign in and try to find friends who already had accounts. The difference with Thefacebook was that you weren't looking across an ocean of humanity trying to find the few people whom you actually knew. Instead, you were just searching through an online representation of the real-life social network at your school.

In addition, people were probably treating invitations to join Thefacebook differently. If your email inbox suddenly had four or five invitations to connect on Thefacebook, and these invitations were coming from people you knew were much more connected on campus than you were, your odds of joining the network were already much higher.

The team at Thefacebook also put the majority illusion to work when targeting certain schools to expand into.[20] In fact, their tactic looked like one straight out of Tim Ferriss's playbook (or better said, Ferriss took from their playbook, because they were doing it first). If a targeted school resisted their expansion, or if a rival website had already begun to take root, they wouldn't just compete directly. Instead, they would open the service up to that school and as many other schools in that school's area as possible.

For example, when they wanted to take root at Baylor University, they found that the school had a similar and homegrown service already in place. So Thefacebook suddenly opened up at the University of Texas at Arlington, Texas A&M, and Southwestern University to form basically a circle around Baylor's hometown of Waco, Texas. The intention was to create outside peer pressure. Popular and connected students from their high school years would be able to reach out to their friends at Baylor and invite them to join. Again, the majority illusion would go to work, this time creating pressure not just to join but to eventually abandon the old service as well.

Eventually, Facebook (now having dropped the "the," and the front-runner among all online social network services) opened up to everyone, not just college students on specific campuses. But to give the majority illusion credit, this happened only after a huge number of users had signed on and the initial early adopters had graduated into the larger world. That critical mass of users was likely even large enough to keep up a majority—or at least plurality—illusion among tech-savvy twenty-somethings now in the workforce.

Whether you are trying to sell a product or seeking the attention of a critical potential contact, the lesson of the majority "illusion" is exactly that: largely unknown companies, brands, and even people can appear to have big followings if they target the right early adopters. That illusion of majority preference then becomes a self-fulfilling prophecy and can turn the unknown into the well known.

FROM SCIENCE TO PRACTICE

The majority illusion is a quirk of perspective, but it's one that can be hugely beneficial if you are trying to make a key connection. Individuals often look first to the most connected people in the local network to make quick estimates about what is popular and who is influential. If you are looking for an introduction to someone specific, the research on the majority illusion suggests that it is best not to rely on just one person you may know to make the connection.

Instead, study the network around that target for other connections. See how many mutual connections you already have, and consider who among them may be the better people to ask for an introduction. You may still rely on just one individual to make a specific introduction, but you can also prepare other mutual connections by sharing your intent to connect with them and asking if they would be willing to put in a good word for you or at least say something nice if asked. In the end, if multiple people in a target's close network are all talking about you, and if the most connected and trusted person is making the introduction, there is a much better chance that you will make the connection.

Practicing Online

In the social media era, the majority illusion becomes even more important. If you are a total stranger asking to be connected to someone who may be a key figure in your industry or organization, always expect that target person to do some research first and expect that research to be done online. You are probably going to get Googled, and your social media profiles are going to get searched, especially for mutual connections. Luckily, social media is also how you are probably going to find out the best way to connect with that person. Looking him or her up on Facebook or LinkedIn will show several mutual connections and that information is important for mapping out the network and how the majority illusion might be created. Importantly, it will also tell you if that illusion is impossible. If you have no mutual connections and really have only friend-of-friend-of-friend pathways between you, then it's likely that the time isn't right to make that connection. Better to wait until your own network is further developed. (As you wait and grow your network, you might even find that the connection happens naturally.)

For a downloadable template to use when completing this exercise, go to http://davidburkus.com/resources/ and look for networking resources.

— 9 —

RESIST HOMOPHILY

Or
Why Opposites
Rarely Attract

We tend to assume that having a large and expansive network automatically means we will have a collection of diverse perspectives to rely on for information. However, recent research shows that people in networks tend to gravitate toward like-minded people and that most of the people we are likely to meet are already thinking like us. This means that simply trying to meet more and more people won't work to give us the range of information we need in order to make better decisions and find better opportunities. In fact, this approach can even lead to making disastrous choices.

On November 8, 2016, Donald Trump shocked America. Well, Donald Trump shocked half of America.

Sometime around 9:20 p.m., US Eastern time, the predictions of pollsters, data scientists, and media pundits changed dramatically.[1] For almost the entire campaign season, including most of Election Day, the consensus was that Trump's opponent, Hillary Rodham Clinton, was going to win the election and become the country's first female president. As the results started coming in from more and more counties, particularly those in the Midwestern "Rust Belt" states, Trump's chances began looking better and better. By midnight, the forecasters who that morning had been assured of Clinton's victory now gave Trump more than a 90 percent probability of winning.[2] At 1:39 a.m., the Associated Press forecasted that Trump would win the state of Pennsylvania. The next moment, Nate Silver, founder of the politics forecasting website Fivethirtyeight.com and the forecaster who correctly predicted the outcome in forty-nine out of fifty states in 2008 and all fifty in 2016, replied to this news: "The AP has essentially called the presidency for Trump."[3]

About an hour later, Silver, who that morning had given Trump only a 28.6 percent chance of winning,[4] would post on his website: "That's a wrap. Donald Trump has been elected president of the United States."[5] While Silver was careful to explain that the polling had shown a competitive race and that Clinton had a few weaknesses in the Electoral College, he called the result "the most shocking political development of my lifetime."[6]

To be sure, Nate Silver was not the only one who was shocked. The majority of forecasters had favored Clinton to win, and most with a greater assertion of certainty than Silver's.[7] Prediction markets had favored Clinton, as did the majority of public relations and communications professionals surveyed by *PRWeek* magazine.[8] The *New York Times* claimed weeks before the election that Clinton was "poised to win easily."[9] Just a few weeks before Election Day, Harvard University professors were assuming a Clinton win and discussing how to "build an exit ramp" for Trump supporters, already tackling the challenge of deescalating the blowback among Trump's voters.[10] Longtime Democratic House leader Nancy Pelosi went even further, claiming as early as June and with great confidence that the Democrats would "win it all," referring to Democrats' chances of recapturing the Senate and earning more seats in the House of Representatives. Pelosi called candidate Trump "the gift that keeps giving to us."[11] Even inside of the Clinton campaign, the consensus on Election Day was that victory was a sure thing, and Clinton campaign aides were popping bottles of champagne on the campaign plane early in the day on Tuesday.[12] It seemed like everyone was telling everyone else that Clinton's victory was a sure thing.

In the aftermath of the election, one of the most common emotions among those disappointed by the election results was sheer shock. "The outcome was so certain; how could the reality be anything different? How could we have missed this when everyone we knew was assuring a Clinton victory?" Some even went as far as to wonder how Trump could win when no one they knew had voted for him.[13] Despite the shock and surprise, however, signs of a Trump victory were definitely present. They just weren't noticed.

The Clinton campaign even had warnings about the Rust Belt and about the state of Michigan in particular. But those warnings were so soft and so few that they were largely ignored. A week and a half away from Election Day, the Service Employees International Union started hearing reports of worry on the ground in Michigan.[14] The union leaders decided to pull volunteers from campaigning in Iowa and move them to Detroit to shore up efforts there. But even as they were booking hotel rooms, the headquarters of Clinton's campaign told them to remain in Iowa. The campaign team was certain they would win Michigan by five percentage points.

Not that the entire campaign team was so certain, actually. Jake Sullivan, Clinton's policy director, was the sole member of the inner circle who expressed concerns that she might lose.[15] Sullivan tried often to convince the rest of the team to devote more time and attention to Michigan and the other Midwestern swing states. Sullivan's concerns weren't rejected . . . they were just ignored. The inner circle was too busy deciding what traditionally Republican states they wanted to add to their winnings. The overwhelming opinion of the network of Democratic campaigners was that Michigan, and the entire election, was in the bag.

To be sure, most of the Trump campaign's data and expectations pointed to only an outside chance of winning, but they were cautiously optimistic.[16] But the race was certainly far closer than it appeared to a huge portion of the population. On the day of the election, RealClearPolitics, which keeps an aggregate of polls at both the national and statewide levels, was showing Clinton winning by only two Electoral College votes, and many of the states in the Democrat's corner were well within the margin of error of polling.[17] Clearly, many people were seeing only the result that they wanted to see.

Perhaps the most famous Election Day prediction that turned out to be correct was from the liberal activist and filmmaker Michael Moore. Months before Election Day, before either Trump or Clinton had even been officially nominated by their party, Moore said in an interview, "I know that they [the Trump campaign] are planning to focus on Michigan, Ohio, Pennsylvania, and Wisconsin. That's how he can win the election . . . If he can get those upper kind of Midwestern-type states, then he can pull it off." A few months later, in July, Moore had strengthened his assertion: he insisted that Trump would win.

His assertion proved true. Though it took time for the election results to be final, in the end Trump won Ohio, Pennsylvania, Wisconsin, and even Michigan. But how did Moore foresee this while so many others did not? For starters, Moore is from Michigan, and he still lives and works there. His early film work focused on the economic plight of the working class in Michigan and other Rust Belt states. While so many other pundits cited demographic and other changes that were making the Rust Belt working class somewhat irrelevant, Moore had firsthand experience of just how strong a force that blue-collar group could be in the general election. But his prediction was either not taken seriously or, if it was, discredited.

In the shocked aftermath of the election, members of the American media began to wonder how they had missed the trend —and why people like Michael Moore saw it. Over time the consensus developed that, indeed, they didn't understand how to interpret events and data because of their own isolation from opposing views.

There were warning signs. Months before Election Day, *New York Times* columnist David Brooks (a conservative who still gave Trump little to no chance of winning the nomination) offered an explanation of why even Trump's nomination was unpredictable. Brooks wrote, "We expected Trump to fizzle because we were not socially intermingled with his supporters and did not listen carefully enough."[18] Brooks was the first journalist, but not the last, to acknowledge not being engaged enough with opposing sides to understand their viewpoints or to notice the signs of Trump's campaign momentum. Margaret Sullivan, a media columnist for the *Washington Post,* admitted, "We didn't take them seriously. Or not seriously enough."[19] Two days after the election, *CBS News* political correspondent Will Rahn admitted that "we also missed the story, after having spent months mocking the people who had a better sense of what was going on."[20]

Meanwhile, Michael Moore had a front-row seat on what was going on in what he considered his hometown. Others were too geographically or ideologically isolated to harbor any doubt. But how could such isolation happen? Is there really a connection between where you live and not only how you see the world but how you think the rest of the world sees itself? The evidence suggests that there is indeed a strong connection. And it affects all of us.

In the early 2000s, the journalist Bill Bishop and the sociology professor Rob Cushing began researching what appears to be an intriguing trend: neighborhoods were becoming increasingly more conservative or liberal.[21] This wasn't just people migrating to liberal or conservative states. Rather, this was happening inside of states, inside of cities themselves, where people appeared to be sorting themselves into neighborhoods based on their ideology.

Bishop and Cushing both live in Austin, Texas, a fairly liberal enclave in a mostly conservative state. They began collecting data on presidential voting records and sorting it by county. Right away the evidence seemed to back up their hunch. Across more than 3,100 counties, a pattern emerged. From 1948 to 1976, Democrats and Republicans were fairly evenly mixed and over that period became even more so. But after the 1976 election, things got very different, very quickly. Migration patterns showed that people began to sort themselves out, and that Democrat and Republican counties began to emerge—they were growing more segregated.

For example, during the polarizing and hotly contested race between Richard Nixon and Hubert Humphrey in 1968, just 37.2 percent of voters lived in a landslide county (places where one candidate won the county by more than 20 percent of the vote). By the year 2000, that number had risen to 45.3 percent.[22] Overall, from 1976 to 2004, the gap between the parties at the county level increased in over 2,000 counties, while only about 1,000 counties grew more competitive. This sorting was not just long-distance migration either. It wasn't people moving to "red" states or "blue" states. Even inside of states, people were migrating to those counties where they felt more comfortable politically.

In California, a traditionally blue state, thirty counties became more solidly Republican, while only eleven counties grew more contested.[23] The same thing happened in the other direction. In San Francisco County, 44 percent of voters sided with Gerald Ford in 1976, but by 2004 only 15 percent of voters went Republican. Meanwhile, the number of voters in the county overall hadn't changed—but for every Republican who left a Democrat moved in.

Bishop and Cushing even examined whether or not gerrymandering—the practice of redrawing congressional districts to gain an advantage—was at play.[24] Interestingly, most of the studies they found suggested that partial redistricting actually made incumbent politicians less safe, not more so. There was no observable change in competitive districts immediately following any redistricting for the last three decades they studied. In short, politicians weren't redrawing boundaries to pick their voters; voters were moving inside of new boundaries to pick their politicians. "Most of America and most Americans were engaged in a thirty-year movement toward more homogenous ways of living," Bishop wrote, no doubt baffled by the patterns he saw.[25]

The Big Social Network Sort

But to a network scientist, this pattern isn't baffling at all. Instead, it is the exact footprint you would expect from the march of homophily. In networks, opposites don't attract. Like-minded people do.

Originally coined by Paul Lazarsfeld and Robert Merton in the 1950s, *homophily* illustrates with data the old adage, "Birds of a feather flock together."[26] In personal relationships, the theory predicts that we are more likely to develop close ties with people who are like us. In social networks, it asserts that networks of individuals will inherently become more segregated and clustered over time. And in study after study, the effect is well documented. Sociologists have seen it wherever they look, from marriages to coworkers to social acquaintances and, yes, even to politics. Homophily on a large scale helps explain the mass migrations that Bishop and Cushing noticed—what they called the "big sort."

But when it comes to political persuasions, homophily affects not just decisions on where to live but also choices of whom to listen to and what to read. In October 2008, the organizational analyst Valdis Krebs analyzed the network of book purchases on Amazon.com, using data on the books that customers bought as connection points.[27] While the network that he analyzed focused on books and the ideas therein, not on actual people, you have to remember that it's people who buy books, not ideas. His analysis revealed a stark separation of book purchases into not just two but three different clusters. People who bought books about Republican ideas weren't connected at all to those who bought books about Democratic ideas. Even more surprising, the people buying Democratic books weren't connected to those buying books about Barack Obama. While Krebs's analysis foreshadowed Obama's ability to stitch together a winning coalition of voters, it also foreshadowed the difficulties he would have working with Congress as president.

Sociologists and network scientists have observed the presence of homophily for a long time, but few have found a way to study what triggers it. It's logical that people form relationships with others whose thinking is similar to their own, because maintaining such a relationship is much easier. But it's also just as logical that something else is at play. Consider that people tend to choose their friends and even their favored coworkers from a fairly limited pool of the people around them (for example, the people they work with, or the friends of friends they already have). So it could also be that similarities in relationships are a result of locations in a social network. Or it could be both.

It was exactly that question that Duncan Watts (yes, the same Duncan Watts) and the graduate student Gueorgi Kossinets sought to answer. To begin, they needed a network—and a large one—to study. In addition, it had to be a network they could observe over time, since it's kind of hard to study the origins of something just by looking at a brief snapshot in time. This was a puzzle that previous researchers had struggled to solve. But fortunately for Kossinets and Watts, new technologies offered a solution. Just as we learned from studies of structural holes, Kossinets and Watts believed that email data could be used to draw a rough picture of the connections inside an organization or community. "Reciprocated emails for the most part represent real relationships," Watts wrote. "It is possible to use email exchanges as a way to observe underlying social networks."[28]

Together, they collected data on more than 30,000 students, faculty, and staff at a large university in the United States over the course of an academic year.[29] They collected not just the logs of email communication but also data on individual attributes (such as gender, age, department, years in the community) and also records of course registrations (not just courses that students took but also the courses that faculty taught). In total, they collected over 7 million message records—and that was after filtering out all messages sent to more than one person.

By taking all this data together, Kossinets and Watts were able to construct a model of the social network and show how it changed over the course of 270 days (the academic year). In particular, they were focused on new ties that formed over time in the network. Using this model, they found something remarkable.

Homophily did indeed predict who formed a tie with whom. People who were similar to each other but were not acquainted were far more likely than dissimilar people to form a connection over time. However, they found that where someone was positioned in the overall social network of the university also had an effect. Most often, individuals who were close to each other in the structure of the social network were already more similar to each other than distant pairs even before establishing a relationship. Taken together, the effect of where you sit in the network —that is, your proximity to potential connections—appears to influence your choice of who you connect with more than pure similarity.

Over time, what Kossinets and Watts observed was a weak preference for similar individuals made stronger by the way the network structure gradually changed to bring similar people closer together and more likely to form a connection. Their results suggest that homophily is a downward spiral. *Small initial preferences matter, but how they change future choices strengthens the appearance of a preference for similarity.*

The results also shed light on just how puzzling the problem of homophily turns out to be. Staying tightly clustered inside a network of similar voices, opinions, and characteristics can truly limit your ability to get an accurate picture of the environment around you and to make the best decisions for yourself or your organization. But that same tightly clustered network also makes it more and more difficult to find the new voices, opinions, and characteristics you need to obtain a more accurate picture. The bottom line is that who you know affects how you think, and it also affects which friend of a friend you're likely to meet, for better or worse.

Diversity Is a Network Problem

For the leaders of Gimlet Media, the fear was that homophily's effects would be for the worse. Gimlet Media is the experiment of Alex Blumberg and his cofounder, Matt Lieber. Alex was a longtime veteran of public radio, having worked as a producer of the hit show *This American Life* and also as a cofounder of *Planet Money,* one of the original National Public Radio (NPR) podcasts. Working on *Planet Money* made Blumberg attuned to the emerging market for podcasts and downloadable audio (usually nonfiction stories or interviews) that could be consumed on demand. But he also saw that listeners would support it. After *Planet Money* raised over half a million dollars for a T-shirt (and documented the making of that T-shirt in a series of episodes), he had an idea.[30] As he studied it more and more, he became convinced that listener commitment was indicative of a big opportunity. NPR is a nonprofit, journalism-focused organization, but he knew that a few for-profit companies were doing really well in podcasting. NPR shows like *This American Life* and *RadioLab* were also dominating the podcast market, despite being aired on radio as well.

Would the market respond well to a for-profit podcasting company built with the same kind of attention to quality that NPR shows had become known for? There was only one way to find out.

In August 2014, Blumberg started a podcast—appropriately titled *Startup*. It was a podcast about starting a podcast company, which he originally called American Podcasting Corporation (a nod to American Broadcasting Company, or ABC), though he and his cofounder quickly changed the name to Gimlet after working with a branding firm on an episode of the show itself. (The name is essentially meaningless, besides being a gin cocktail.) Both the show and the company grew quickly, as Blumberg and Lieber raised $1.5 million in investment from venture capital firms.[31] They even raised an additional $200,000 in investment by appealing to listeners of the show who were accredited investors and wanted to be a part of their adventure.[32] The investment money fueled more growth projects, and they quickly added two new shows.

That fueled additional interest, in both listeners and investors. After Gimlet received another $6 million in investment in 2015, the company was valued at $30 million.[33] That much larger investment meant they needed to spur much larger growth. And growth meant more listeners and more shows; new shows meant more people. But as they looked at their current staff and started planning for their future staff, they noticed something they didn't like.

In December 2015, the same month they received their $6 million investment, their office was pretty uniform and pretty white. They had twenty-seven employees at the time, and twenty-four of them were white. True to their unique style of transparency, the team at Gimlet decided to make a podcast about it. It was on the show that Blumberg stated why this lack of diversity was so troubling. "We have an obligation to do right by the stories we'll be telling," he said. "To tell them not just from one perspective, but with all the nuance and complexity they deserve."[34]

To explore the issue, not only for the podcast but also for themselves, Blumberg interviewed several Gimlet employees, especially the employees of color. Despite the potentially uncomfortable experience of "three people of color bravely diving into a sometimes awkward conversation with their white CEO about race and diversity," Blumberg learned just how easy it is to fall into a homogenous company roster and just how homogenous theirs was.[35]

It was during an interview with an openly gay colleague that a more interesting question arose. Beyond their surface-level diversity problem, did Gimlet lack ideological diversity? "The vast majority of the staff is sorta like politically liberal, cosmopolitan leaning, you know sort of like Brooklyn-based," Blumberg told his colleague, but they didn't appear to be political or religiously diverse. "We don't have any Evangelicals on staff . . . I don't think we have anyone who can name one NASCAR driver."[36] At that moment during the interview, the producer, sitting outside the booth listening to the conversation, walked in and asked if he could join the conversation. He was an Evangelical. He went to church every Sunday. He could even name a few NASCAR drivers. And he often felt like the only one; he felt like it was better to keep all of this to himself.

After that interview, Blumberg started to really understand the complexity of their problem. Their goal was clear: "We want to make sure that Gimlet is a place where you feel comfortable sharing your beliefs. Be you Christian, Native American, or transgender, or all of the above," he said.[37] At the same time, Blumberg recognized that the environment and the social network that his company operated inside of were going to make it tough for that to happen.

"We are a largely white organization in a historically pretty white industry," he continued. "If we just sit around and wait for people of color to apply for the jobs we post, we are going to stay that way."[38] In fact, when they looked at their hiring methods, they found that they were pulling from a homogenous pool, since they mostly relied on refugees from the world of public radio to apply or recruited them directly. Like the university in Kossinets and Watts's study, they didn't have a strong preference for similarity, but their place in the larger social network was serving similarity as the only option.

In fact, most of the diverse hires up to that point had come from deliberately acting differently—going out of their way to connect with people from a much different industry or section of the network. They learned that this would be their best chance of solving their dilemma. "A more diverse staff means that there are more professional networks to tap into, and the process of becoming less monochromatic as an organization can take on momentum," Blumberg said.[39]

Blumberg's internal investigation shows just how hard diversity can be. Just as Kossinet and Watts's study showed that homophily is a downward spiral, you may start out with a preference to connect with similar people, but that shapes your network, making it easier and easier to keep choosing the same type of people. If Gimlet succeeds as a company, whether or not they manage to break free of the temptation to select from a homogenous pool will likely have been a contributing factor.

Opposites don't attract; similar people do. But when similar people connect, they change the broader social network to make more similar connections more probable. Kossinet and Watts's study also suggests, however, that it's possible to reverse course and become an upward spiral. It suggests we can break free from homophily by putting to work the same principles that drive it. Deliberately seeking out new, dissimilar connections moves your place in the network and makes it more likely that your future connections will also be dissimilar. The lesson of homophily is that who you know affects how you think. Because you're most likely to know people who think like you do, it takes deliberate work to move against the strong current of similarity, but the benefits of escaping that current are legion.

FROM SCIENCE TO PRACTICE

The biggest implication from homophily research is that we are much more likely to make, and to already have, connections with people who are similar to us. While that's good for making us feel comfortable, it's bad for making decisions with lots of variables. We need our network to give us alternative perspectives, and to do that we need to know if our network has any alternative perspectives. We need to do an audit of our network.

So here is a quick exercise for doing just that:

1. Take a look at your most frequent interactions in a given week. Use the call records on your phone or your email outbox to generate a list of twenty to twenty-five people.
2. Add those names to the first column of a list, with your name at the top.
3. Then make a few more columns alongside your name and label each column with the category you want to audit—industry, department, function, race, religion, political ideology, etc.
4. Start listing where each person in the first column fits in those categories. If you don't know, take a guess and then go find out. (You are probably wrong more often than you suspect.)

Chances are that, for all categories, many of your contacts are going to be pretty similar to you. And that should give you an idea of what you need to work on.

Practicing Online

If most of your connections are active on social media, you can fill out this list even faster. Odds are that their profiles include much of this information. Services like LinkedIn, for example, should have individuals' job and education information, as well as the groups they belong to. Services like Facebook should show you what things your connections "like." You might be tempted to disconnect with them after seeing some of these things, but don't . . . if these connections are different from you, you probably need them in your life even more than you think.

For a downloadable template to use when completing this exercise, go to http://davidburkus.com/resources/ and look for networking resources.

— 10 —

SKIP MIXERS — SHARE ACTIVITIES INSTEAD

Or

Why the Best Networking Events Have Nothing to Do with Networking

The most common association we have with connections and networking is networking events, those special places and times dedicated to meeting new people. As with homophily, however, we are most likely to use our time at such events to connect with people we already know or people who are similar to ourselves. Networking events don't bring us truly new contacts. Instead, research suggests, we are better off engaging in activities that draw a cross-section of people and letting those connections form naturally as we engage with the task at hand.

IF YOU ARE INVITED to dinner at the home of Jon Levy, you can count on two things. The first is that you will be doing the cooking. The second is that you will be shocked at who is cooking alongside you.

"The big joke is that one day I hope to do something great enough to be worthy of an invite to my own dinner," Levy says often.[1] The reason for the do-it-yourself cooking, the remarkable attendees, and even the joke is that, for the better part of a decade, Jon Levy's home has been host to a secret, invite-only dining experience attended by some of the most influential people in the world. That would include famous comedians, award-winning musicians, best-selling authors, television personalities, Nobel Prize laureates, and even royalty. Levy's home and the dinners themselves have created one of the most impactful communities in the world—and an equally impactful network for Levy.

The dinner routine follows a strict format. It begins with invitations. Each guest receives a fairly vague email from Levy's assistant inviting them to an event called "the Influencers Dinner." Levy is most often a stranger to the guests at the time of the invitation. (However, the guests have often been referred to Levy by his former dinner attendees.) Levy has also ensured, as best he can, that none of the invited guests have met each other before.

Upon arrival at Levy's Upper West Side home in New York City or at one of the venues in other cities where he hosts dinners, guests are informed that they will be cooking their dinner together and are broken up into teams. The meal preparation is not complicated; no cooking experience is required. What is required, however, is strict adherence to one rule: as they prepare the meal, no one is allowed to talk about who they are or what they do for a living. Guests are only allowed to use their first names and are not allowed to make any other inquiries about each other's names. Yet despite this rule, participants bond quickly, and the crowd of strangers becomes a room of fast friends.

When the meal is ready, participants sit down to eat and play a quick game. One by one, the diners take turns guessing each other's real identity and profession. This game of delightful surprises—where finding out you are wrong is almost more fun than guessing correctly—occupies most of dinner. When it's over, everyone pitches in to do the dishes. Often the small dinner opens up to a larger gathering as previous dinner guests arrive for a cocktail party and salon that follows. That party can last into the early hours of the following morning and has been known to include world-class magicians performing illusions, world-renowned musicians sitting down at the piano and leading a sing-along, and thought leaders and scientists sharing their latest discoveries.

After years of conducting dinners (over 120 and counting), Levy has built a community of over 1,000 dinner guests, all of whom, whether they are famous or not, are influencing society. "There's only a loose connection between being famous and being influential," Levy explained. "The stylist for a couple of well-known celebrities probably has more influence on the fashion industry than the celebrities themselves."[2]

But it's the network that is the true goal of these dinners, according to Levy. He believes that bringing together a community of diverse, influential people will almost inevitably lead to new partnerships and collaborations that make a positive impact on the world. And he's got proof to back up that belief. Levy's community has launched start-ups, produced television shows, and even kindled a few romantic relationships. The network has also made a positive impact on Levy's career.

Levy developed the initial idea for the Influencers Dinner between 2008 and 2009. He was attending a seminar when the program leader shared his belief that "the fundamental element that defines the quality of our lives are the people we surround ourselves with and the conversations we have with them."[3] That remark triggered something in Levy. He was no stranger to the power of interactions and to gatherings of influential people. He had a solid job, working as a digital marketing consultant for a variety of companies. But when Levy examined his own life in the light of that statement, he realized that his experiences weren't quite as extraordinary as he might have hoped.

He started small, spending almost a year thinking about the exact format a community event would take. With a professional background in the study of behavioral science and influence, he knew that the details of the event would dramatically affect the outcome. He also started with a smaller guest list, at least in terms of influence. The first few dinners were mostly just his influential friends and their referrals, but even then he was reaching for influencers on a larger scale. "Often I would just embarrass myself because I didn't know how to communicate with people who operate at that level, and so it was a bit of a train wreck at times," Levy said. "I just kept doing it and doing it and learning how to express it better and more effectively each time."[4]

But to create the best experience with a guest list of ever more accomplished people, Levy also realized that he would need to tweak the format of his dinners. "Everyone was too accomplished," he said. "The moment they started talking about their careers, they would act overly important and it would lack the experience, community, and bonding that I was hoping for," Levy reflected. That's how the rule that would come to define his dinners was born. Levy insisted going forward that no one could share who they were or what they did until sitting down to dinner. "As a result, everyone has to drop their perfectly rehearsed introduction and learn how to connect without giving away their normal role."[5]

Levy believes that the secrecy also changes the behavior of attendees for the better. "When people don't know your traditional role, there's no expectation about how you should act," he believes.[6] And when attendees act less like they think people expect them to, they act more like themselves and form a more cohesive network.

Since starting the Influencers Dinners, Levy's own career has grown immensely. The network he's built has provided him with job opportunities, an expanding consulting business, a book deal, and numerous speaking gigs. But to Levy, none of this came from trying to extract value from the network. Instead, it's the result of trying to invest more and more value into the Influencers community.

Elsewhere in New York City (elsewhere in the Upper West Side actually), entrepreneur Chris Schembra is doing something similar, but a bit differently. Like Levy, he's found that he has a passion for connecting others and that hosting dinners serves as the group activity that works best. Schembra's 450-square-foot studio apartment, with furniture pushed up against the walls, serves as the venue for his "747 Club" dinners.

Schembra's dinners take place at a small table with paper plates and plastic cups. Needless to say, guests cook and eat in close quarters, but they form close connections as well. The events started from a realization that he wanted to build a better network, that the best way to do that was by building a community—and that he could cook a delicious pasta sauce. "I invited fifteen of my friends to my home, fed them my sauce," Schembra said. "I delegated tasks and empowered them to be a part of the process. They liked it, and they liked meeting each other."[7]

Cooking isn't the only aspect of the process that Schembra's guests are empowered to be a part of. "Every minute for three hours is perfectly placed and structured," Schembra said. When they arrive at his home, Schembra greets guests at the door and welcomes them into a completely open apartment, with no tables or chairs in sight. There are just some guests, drinks, and a few hors d'oeuvres. But it's all part of the plan. When the last guest arrives, the dinner prep begins. Schembra starts boiling the water and assigns specific tasks. Guests not only help with cooking and making dessert but set up the table, lay out place settings, and (most importantly) begin to talk to each other as they work together. The name 747 Club comes from Schembra's meticulous attention to the steps involved. "It takes thirteen minutes to cook three and a half boxes of pasta al dente," Schembra said.[8] Dinner is always served at 8:00 p.m., so cooking starts at 7:47. By the time dinner is served, Schembra has structured a series of activities to ensure that no one is sitting next to a stranger.

The conversation continues for about twenty-five to thirty minutes, at which point Schembra turns up the heat a bit more. "At 8:32, I stand up and I tell a joke, to lighten everyone up, but then I transition into sharing something more personal, which gets them comfortable with being vulnerable." He shares a piece of his own story, taking the first step toward being vulnerable, and then facilitates the conversation as it travels around the table and everyone shares—usually something remarkably personal given that it's only been ninety minutes since everyone there met for the first time. "I consider it a failure if I don't see at least two people cry during a dinner," Schembra joked, a reflection of how quickly bonds are made during these dinners—every time. "The feelings generated don't change regardless of who is at the table. That impact is a scalable product."[9]

And scale it has. From the sixteen-person dinners with friends and friends of friends, Schembra has scaled the 747 Club dinners into a variety of shapes and sizes for corporate clients. He has taken the format, and the same pasta sauce recipe, on the road and organizes team-building and connection-fostering events for a variety of companies. Typically, a corporate 747 Club format is a series of individual small dinners over several nights, followed by a large salonlike event where individuals reconnect with their fellow dinner guests and trade stories about their experience with guests from the previous nights' dinners. Since 2015, Schembra and the 747 Club have fed over 3,000 people and sparked more than 100,000 relationships. Beyond corporate clients, attendees at Schembra's personal dinners have grown into a community of their own and even refer new members. "The first time you come, you come alone," Schembra said. "The second time, bring a friend. After that, you're eligible to nominate a new guest."[10]

Jon Levy and Chris Schembra designed their dinners through trial and error, but insights from social science reveal why their dinners work so well and why they have created unlikely communities across all sorts of unlikely sectors, with these two hosts at the center of the network. While sharing meals has been a part of the human experience for thousands of years, more recent research suggests that it's not just compiling a remarkable guest list and breaking bread that's bringing people together.

It's the cooking.

Working Together Brings People Together

To fully appreciate why forcing attendees to cook their own dinner brings them closer together, we first have to examine what doesn't work when trying to make network connections and then revisit an old idea in its smaller form. What doesn't work for making network connections is exactly what so many people rely on for meeting new people: traditional networking events.

Most people have been to a networking event or mixer—a group of people standing around high cocktail tables, talking to each other and hoping to make just the right connection. To an introvert, these events are terrifying, but it turns out that these events aren't all that effective for extroverts either. Research suggests that mixers, parties, events, and even regular dinners that attempt to foster new relationships work poorly for precisely the same reason they were designed to work well: new relationships.

In other words, when we focus solely on networking or meeting new contacts, we most often end up heading home from these events with far less useful relationships than we had hoped for.

The reason for this is what the network science researcher Brian Uzzi calls the *self-similarity principle*. Uzzi (whom you've met in previous chapters and will meet again) asserts that when we are seeking to make new contacts, we tend to choose people who disproportionately are very similar to ourselves, whether in terms of job type, industry, experience, training, worldview, or something else. If this sounds a bit like the phenomenon of homophily, that's because it is essentially homophily in a smaller form. It's the micro-homophily that drives so much of the macro-homophily we see when we look across an entire network. According to Uzzi, we tend toward self-similarity for two reasons: *comfort* and *efficiency*. It's easier to put our trust in people whose worldview is similar to our own, and it's easier to feel comfortable with these people because they will not challenge our worldview. It's also far more efficient to have a conversation with people whose backgrounds are similar to ours, as we mutually recognize concepts, analogies, and other jargon. While comfort and efficiency are important, the problem is that chasing either or both yields relationships that are far less likely to provide us with new information or challenge our thinking about issues. If our network doesn't think that differently from us, then we won't be pushed to expand our thinking or to question our reasoning. Self-similarity gives us positive feedback even when that's not what we may need.

In addition to our tendency to choose new relationships with people who are similar to ourselves, we also have a tendency at networking events to gravitate toward existing relationships. In a notable study of networking events from Columbia Business School professors Paul Ingram and Michael Morris, those executives who claimed to desire more opportunities to meet new contacts most often failed to utilize those opportunities as much as hoped. The researchers organized a networking mixer as part of the executive MBA program at Columbia. Many of those invited were students who had actually been lobbying Columbia to put on more social events as part of the curriculum, so that they could benefit from the rich and diverse network of colleagues. In total, about 100 executives, consultants, entrepreneurs, and bankers gathered together for food and drinks on a Friday evening. Prior to the event, Ingram and Morris surveyed the executives to learn who among the invited guests they already knew and what their intentions and objectives were for the event. Besides having fun, 95 percent of the attendees said they wanted to meet new people during the event.

When they arrived, the researchers outfitted each attendee with an nTag, a small electronic device that registered each conversation and tracked how long it lasted. Besides being asked not to remove the nTag, attendees were told: "Act normally. Talk to whomever you want to, while enjoying food and drinks."[11] The attendees did just that. Unfortunately, the "whomever" they liked talking to tended mostly to be people they already knew. Despite knowing an average of only one-third of the people in the room, the executives spent about half of their conversations talking to people they were already friendly with.

While it's encouraging that they spent the other half of their time having conversations with new people, that percentage is far short of their previously stated intent. Even taking a random approach should have yielded more conversations with new contacts than most of the executives actually had. In addition, those new conversations tended to be with others who were most like themselves. That is, the consultants talked to consultants, and the bankers talked to bankers. In terms of both new conversations and diverse connections, the most successful networker at the event turned out to be the bartender.

If even the best-intentioned executives failed to meet enough new people, clearly the pull of self-similarity is strong. So how can we avoid that pull? It turns out that the best strategy might be to just stop trying to meet new people. Instead, we are more likely to develop new relationships with a diverse set of individuals by focusing more on activities to participate in rather than relationships themselves. Like guests cooking alongside each other, participating in shared activities allows more random collaborations to happen and makes those collaborations more likely to become real relationships. Brian Uzzi also has a term for this phenomenon: he calls it the *shared activities principle*.

Based on Uzzi's nearly 100 sociological and social network studies, the shared activities principle states that "powerful networks are not forged through casual interactions but through sharing in high-stakes activities that bring together a diverse set of participants."[12] In other words, *schmoozing at a mixer is far less likely to lead you to a powerful network than jumping into projects, teams, and activities that draw a diverse set of people together*. One of the primary reasons for this is that, in a shared activity, there is little room to stick to prescribed roles, which makes interactions more genuine. "In sociology, we have a concept I call 'the script,'" Uzzi explained. "In a script, every interaction you have with someone is governed by a certain set of expectations for what is appropriate or inappropriate—about the things you can say and do around the other person."[13] A shared activity allows participants to drop the traditional script, however, and pick up a new one that might be more useful for demonstrating the qualities others need to see to establish a connection. Recall how much more powerful Levy's dinners became once he instituted the "first names only, no talking about work" rule. Levy was forcing dinner guests to leave their scripts at the door.

According to Uzzi, "shared activities are an engine for building these powerful networks rich in social capital."[14] Shared activities stand the best chance of developing potent new network connections when they satisfy three qualities: they evoke passion, they require interdependence, and there is something at stake.

Evoking passion is important because individuals usually find a way to make time for activities they are passionate about. You may not be inclined to go to dinner with strangers, but when your friend raves about a particular dinner and then the host contacts you with an invite, you are much more likely to find the time to go. Interdependence in the activity then speeds up the process of building trust among the guests. You might have your guard up when you arrive, but when you and a random partner are handed utensils and given a task, you pretty quickly realize that you need the other person's cooperation. And having something at stake both heightens that realization of interdependence and provides opportunities for celebration or commiseration. So whether the meal is a success or a failure, sharing a stake in the outcome provides a chance to generate the bonds of loyalty that sustain relationships over time.

As Levy and Schembra have found, it's not the dinner itself—not the sharing of a particular meal or drink—but the act of participating in the meal together that truly generates the connections needed to build a diverse network. Whether it's building a network that helps create opportunities for consulting, research, or other referrals (as in Levy's case) or taking the participatory dining model to companies and helping them build their internal network (as in Schembra's), the shared activity is indeed a potent tactic.

But cooking together isn't the only possible shared activity, and it may not even be the best, depending on your overall objective. Uzzi recommends joining nonprofit boards, volunteering for community service, or even taking up a team sport as potentially vital ways to join a shared activity. Internally, many companies have found that even something as simple as holding classes for employees can draw individuals from across different functions and create a diverse set of new connections. One company may even owe its success to doing just that.

Education as a Shared Activity

Pixar Animation Studios is not your ordinary movie studio. For one thing, it has enjoyed an incredible amount of success considering where it came from, and in a relatively short period of time. When Pixar started, it wasn't even a stand-alone company. It was the computer graphics division of Lucasfilm, and it would have stayed a part of George Lucas's operations had Lucas not been motivated to sell off pieces of his empire. The computer graphics group was purchased by Steve Jobs, who saw the potential for it to become a computer hardware company. The animated films began mostly as a means to make commercials to advertise the power of Pixar products. The films morphed over time, and then, in 1995, Pixar released the critically acclaimed *Toy Story*, the first full-length animated feature film completely drawn from computers.

Since then, the studio has won over 16 Academy Awards and more than 200 other awards, despite making fewer than two dozen feature films. But Pixar's relatively young age and big success alone aren't what makes the studio so unusual; it's also the organizational model. Pixar doesn't operate on the star-centric model of most Hollywood studios. Instead, it treats its entire team as the star; every employee is a vital part of making each film. "Pixar is a community in the true sense of the word," wrote Pixar founder Ed Catmull. "We think that lasting relationships matter. And we share some basic beliefs."[15] One of those beliefs is that ideas for a film don't just come from the director and other creative leaders, but from every single member of the 200 to 250 people working on a film. Another is that building a culture of teamwork, collaboration, and creative success takes deliberate focus.

You can see that focus everywhere at Pixar. For example, the meticulous design of its main building—renamed the Steve Jobs Building in honor of his legacy (and his role in designing the building)—features a huge center atrium that is home to the cafeteria, meeting rooms, employee mailboxes, screening rooms, and even the main bathrooms. (Jobs actually wanted the atrium to house the *only* bathrooms in the building, but that was deemed a bit too extreme.) The design was a deliberate attempt by Jobs to construct a building that would foster truly spontaneous interactions and spark diverse internal networks. And indeed, in the Steve Jobs Building, "you really do have chance encounters at all times," said Catmull.[16]

But while the centralized nature of the main building helps, there's actually a different building on campus that likely makes the biggest contribution to the company's diverse networks and deep teamwork: Pixar University.

Located in the West Village Building (all of the other buildings on campus are named after real places), Pixar University was started fairly early in the company's history, just two years after the release of *Toy Story*. At first, the most in-demand class was a course on drawing. At the time, Pixar had only 120 employees, and 100 of them, from all functions of the company, enrolled in the course. Over time the curriculum grew and morphed. Pixar University has now taught courses in acting, painting, computer programming, improv comedy, juggling, karate, and even belly dancing. Pixar employees are allowed to spend up to four hours of paid work time each week taking courses. They are even allowed to reject meeting requests that conflict with their scheduled course time.[17] And every employee is eligible for the university, regardless of the job they were hired for.

It's allowing anyone in any function to enroll in any course that makes Pixar University such a strong contributor to Pixar's culture and its success. "It wasn't that the class material directly enhanced our employees' job performance," Catmull wrote. "In the classroom setting, people interacted in a way they didn't in the workplace. They felt free to be goofy, relaxed, open, vulnerable."[18] Without knowing about Uzzi's research, Catmull and Pixar established a program that perfectly leveraged the shared activities principle.

The courses bring together a diverse set of employees, all of whom leave their traditional script outside the classroom. "Hierarchy did not apply, and as a result, communication thrived," Catmull wrote.[19] The diversity of the courses offered ensures that those who enroll do so because something about a course evokes a passion in them. And even if employees take courses that may not seem to have much to do with their jobs, Pixar believes that many of the skills they learn are transferable. Teaching accountants or administrative assistants to draw may not seem relevant to Pixar's business success, but a drawing class also teaches students to observe the world more thoroughly—a skill that would increase performance in almost any job.

Pixar University courses also require interdependence. Many of them, like improvisational comedy, require individuals to work together. But even students taking solo courses, like sculpting, benefit from the feedback of other students. "It taught everyone at Pixar, no matter their title, to respect the work that their colleagues did," Catmull wrote. Pixar University courses also teach them that the stakes are always high. "Creativity involves missteps and imperfections," Catmull wrote. "I wanted our people to get comfortable with that idea—that both the organization and its members should be willing, at times, to operate on the edge."[20]

The diverse and unlikely connections made in these courses have a profound impact on Pixar's internal social network. It's not uncommon for two employees to find themselves wrestling or pretending to fight in an improv class, and then to meet the following day in their traditional roles as boss and subordinate. A newly hired technical director once recalled bashing Ed Catmull over the head multiple times with a long red balloon—only to find himself pitching a major business proposal to Catmull a short time later.[21] Pixar University has become one of the major contributors to Pixar's team-based culture, and that culture has led to tremendous success. "Pixar University helps reinforce the mind-set that we're all learning and it's fun to learn together," explained Catmull.[22] While it does so subtly, by leveraging the power of shared activities, other elements of the program are not so subtle. The seal of Pixar University, for example, features the Latin motto *Alienus Non Diutius,* or in English, Alone No Longer.

When most people go about building their network, whether internally in their organization or externally, they seek out events full of new people. But the research on self-similarity, as well as the success of people like Jon Levy and Chris Schembra and organizations like Pixar, suggests that the time spent at networking events and mixers is time wasted. If you want to build a diverse collection of new contacts, your time is better spent engaging in shared activities, especially ones that evoke passion, require interdependence, and put something at stake. You may not even be focused on networking while you participate in such activities, but after you finish, you'll find that you have gathered a host of new and interesting people that now call you friend.

FROM SCIENCE TO PRACTICE

The research on human behavior at networking mixers and on the potency of shared activities is clear: networking events are not especially effective. This is especially good news for the networking-phobic. While these events promise a diverse group of potential new connections, in practice most of us end up clinging to people we already know or new people who are similar to ourselves. What we need instead is to invest time and energy in events and activities that bring the greatest potential for new and diverse connections. The research suggests that our time is better spent seeking out activities with a shared purpose that evokes passion or emotion, requires interdependence, and has something at stake. These shared activities draw a more diverse group of people and create stronger bonds among participants. Here are a few types of shared activities to start participating in:

1. Community service programs
2. Recreational sports leagues, martial arts, or hobby clubs
3. Nonprofit boards or committees
4. At-work special projects teams
5. Churches, synagogues, mosques, and other faith-based groups

Practicing Online

If you are already using many social media services like Facebook and LinkedIn, you are in luck. Many of these services now have "groups" features where like-minded individuals share information, discuss their passions, and collaborate on projects. Be careful not to join groups dedicated solely to networking and connections, since it's likely that a focus on self-similarity will creep in again. Instead, sign up for groups dedicated to your nonwork passions, or at the very least industry groups that are intentionally wide in their reach. Because of the online nature of these groups, many of them draw an even more diverse collection of individuals than in-person activities—and you don't even need to leave your house.

For a downloadable template to use when completing this exercise, go to http://davidburkus.com/resources/ and look for networking resources.

— 11 —

BUILD STRONGER TIES THROUGH MULTIPLEXITY

Or
Why Who You Know Includes How Well You Know Them

When we consider our overall network, we tend to assign people to certain categories. Some are friends, others are business relationships, and still others are people we interact with because of a shared activity. But networks are often much more complicated than such categories suggest. There is a phenomenon that sociologists call multiplexity—that is, two people may have more than one type of relationship. Research reveals that multiplex ties make for a stronger bond between two people, suggesting that, while assigning our contacts to single categories might simplify things, that simplification often comes at a cost of not knowing the full value of our network.

In June 2006, Warren Buffett surprised the philanthropic world by announcing that, while he was still committed to giving away his life fortune to charity, he would not go it alone and just establish a charitable foundation in his own name, as other titans of business traditionally had done (like the Rockefeller Foundation, the Ford Foundation, and others).[1] Instead, he intended to give the bulk of his wealth to the Bill and Melinda Gates Foundation—to pool his resources with those of Bill Gates so that together they could make a bigger impact than either could alone. (However, Buffett did divert some of his wealth to other causes, establishing four charitable trusts named for his late wife and three children.)

To an outside observer, Buffett's move seems quite odd. It was the first time such a large donation wasn't used to set up a namesake foundation. Moreover, Buffett was entrusting the money to someone twenty-five years younger than he was. But those who knew the story of the two men's relationship also knew that Buffett's ability to trust that such a large portion of his wealth would be used effectively and responsibly was based on decades of trust and collaboration. But this is where the story does get odd. Gates and Buffett's relationship was built not on a foundation of doing business together, at least not initially. Instead, it was built on something else.

Playing bridge.

For more than two decades, the two men have strengthened their personal relationship and collaborated on work and philanthropic projects in large part because they shared an affinity for playing the same card game. Gates and Buffett originally met on July 5, 1991. Gates's mother, Mary Maxwell Gates, invited Gates to join her and some friends (including Buffett) for dinner at the family's vacation home. It wasn't the first time Mrs. Gates had entertained notable businesspeople at her home. Nor was it the first time she had used her network and connections to help her son. Mrs. Gates was active in the Seattle philanthropic and business communities, having served as a regent on the University of Washington's board, on the national board of the United Way, and on the boards of several area businesses.[2] It was while she was working with the United Way that Mrs. Gates met John Opel, then chairman of IBM, and encouraged him to work with her son's upstart software company, Microsoft. So when Mrs. Gates hosted these gatherings and invited her son, there was usually a reason.

Nonetheless, Gates didn't want to take time away from working on Microsoft to meet Buffett at first. "He just buys and sells pieces of paper. That's not real value added," Gates told her. "I don't think we'd have much in common."[3] He was wrong. Gates agreed to swing by for a short visit, chatted with Buffett, and almost immediately the two bonded. Buffett asked Gates questions about Microsoft that he had never been asked before. The quick visit turned into hours of conversation—during which they likely uncovered a shared love of bridge.

Since that day, they have grown their friendship and deepened their business relationship, often over a hand of bridge. Most often, the two play online. Gates reportedly uses the name "Chalengr" and Buffett goes by "T-Bone."[4] Buffett estimates that he plays more than 4,000 hands a year online—obviously not all with Gates. Still, the game—and the duo's friendship—has spawned a lot of activity. In 2004, Buffett asked Gates to join the board of Berkshire Hathaway—a position for which he gets paid a mere $2,000 per year. (Berkshire Hathaway directors are the lowest-paid corporate board of any S&P 500 firm.[5]) Less than two years after Gates joined, Buffett announced his donation. Along with the donation, Buffett also joined the Gates Foundation as a trustee to help steer the organization.

Ranging from dinner at Gates's mother's home to countless hands of bridge, to business discussions about the future of Berkshire Hathaway, and eventually to strategizing how best to help the world, Gates and Buffett's relationship is far more complex than it appears on the outside. But the truth is that almost all relationships are. While it's tempting to silo business relationships in one category and personal relationships in another, the reality is that humans connect over a multitude of pathways, mixing business with personal and with myriad other types of connection. Sociologists use the term *multiplexity* to refer to the number of different social connections between any two individuals. And while the discovery of multiplexity is fairly new, its occurrence in business is not.

Consider the strange tale of how the legendary consumer goods company Procter & Gamble got started.[6] William Procter was an English immigrant to America whose first wife had died shortly after they arrived in Cincinnati. He was formally trained as a candlemaker, and while working in a bank by day, he started a one-man candlemaking business that covered everything from manufacturing to sales to delivery. It was in this trade that he met Alexander Norris, the owner of a prominent candle shop in Cincinnati. More importantly, Procter met his daughter, Olivia Norris. Procter quickly proposed to and married Norris. Coincidentally, the Irish immigrant James Gamble was courting Olivia Norris's sister, Elizabeth Ann Norris. Gamble had worked as a soapmaking apprentice and eventually opened his own soap and candle shop. It was both men's new father-in-law, Alexander Norris, who first saw the opportunity. He noticed that both of his new sons-in-law competed for the same raw materials to make their products and suggested that perhaps the two would be better off by simply joining forces. On October 31, 1837, they formally partnered together to form Procter & Gamble.

In the more than one and a half centuries that have passed since the start of their partnership, Procter & Gamble has grown to become one of the largest companies in the world. The company still makes soap and candles, but also medicine, makeup, diapers, and dishwashing liquid. And it all started, not because of the two men's admiration for each other's business savvy, but because of a personal connection that became a multiplex tie.

Fast-forward more than a century and move from the world of soap to the realm of ice cream, and you'll find a similar story. Ice cream legends Ben Cohen and Jerry Greenfield, of Ben & Jerry's, became a multiplex tie and co-ran a multinational corporation from what started as a middle school friendship. "Jerry and I met in junior high," Cohen said. "When he fainted in gym class."[7] The two quickly developed a friendship, partly because they were the slowest two kids running around the track, but also because of their mutual love of food (which likely caused their being the two heaviest and slowest kids in gym class). But in middle school, high school, and even college, starting an ice cream shop wasn't a thought in either of their minds. Instead, they focused on their friendship. Greenfield graduated high school and went to college in Ohio. Cohen went to college in upstate New York but dropped out. He paid a visit to his friend in Ohio and ended up staying for a month, living in Greenfield's dorm room and making money selling sandwiches around the dorms at night.

Cohen moved back to New York City, and after graduation Greenfield took his turn moving into Cohen's apartment. The two grew even more as friends and worked separately to pay the rent. Cohen drove a taxi and tried to sell his pottery; Greenfield tried to get into medical school but ended up working as a lab technician. "Neither of us really liked what we were doing with our lives. So we decided to try to start something together," Cohen said.[8]

They knew they wanted to work with food, and after some research, they settled on ice cream because it had the cheapest equipment costs. Together, they enrolled in a correspondence course on ice cream making. The course cost $5 and featured open-book, open-note tests. "At last we had found a type of education that we really excelled at," Greenfield joked.[9] They chose Burlington, Vermont, as their testing ground because it was a college town without the competition of an existing homemade ice cream store. They fixed up an old gas station, experimented with various recipes and business models, and eventually stumbled onto a winning formula—not just for ice cream but also for business. In 2000, more than two decades after their friendship turned into a business partnership, the pair sold the Ben & Jerry's brand to Unilever for $326 million—a pretty good return on an investment of $5 for an ice cream course.[10]

History is filled with similar examples. While we may want to categorize people into just work and personal buckets, real social networks do not seem to operate that way. And that is to our benefit. Research shows that not only does multiplexity help us become more aware of real-life opportunities, but it enhances our performance on the job—and can even enhance the performance of an entire organization.

The Multiple Opportunities of Multiplexity

Social scientists and network scientists have been studying multiplexity for a number of decades. They have found that a multiplex relationship between individuals dramatically increases trust (presumably because it raises more opportunities to demonstrate trustworthy behavior). It also makes it more likely that new ideas and fresh information will be shared. Compared to those with more uniplex networks, individuals with high degrees of multiplexity in their total network are better able to validate ideas, they have access to greater resources, and they can think more critically and gather more diverse information. As we'll see, multiplex networks may also be able to help an entire organization more than you might think.

In centuries past, when much of the population lived in smaller village societies, multiplexity was pervasive and served as a means to keep groups together; the people you traded with were often also family members, or fellow church parishioners, or at the very least not too distant neighbors.[11] Over time, as populations grew and small villages were transformed into large cities, multiplexity didn't necessarily decrease, but it did shift. The types of multiple ties connecting individuals may have been transformed, but the research shows that humans still tend to gravitate toward certain people for more than one reason, and that the more types of connections there are between two individuals—the higher the multiplexity—the more trust tends to develop in the relationship. In the modern work environment, most often we consider a multiplex relationship as one that combines a work tie and a social tie. This sets up the first question that needs to be answered: which came first, the social tie or the work tie?

It was that precise question that the researchers Simone Ferriani, Fabio Fonti, and Raffaele Corrado sought to answer. Having seen how work and social ties (which they labeled economic and social ties, respectively) can combine to form multiplex connections, the trio decided to study how that multiplexity developed.[12] They focused their research on a cluster of media companies located near Bologna, Italy—two of the three researchers hailed from the University of Bologna. But beyond this convenience, studying such industrial districts is quite smart, since the geographic proximity of the companies made the search for multiplex relationships a much more promising one. After contacting hundreds of firms in advertising, film, publishing, music, and graphic design, the researchers surveyed eighty firms and interviewed either each firm's founder or a cofounder. To find and analyze any multiplexity among these firms (and those that they interacted with), the researchers first had to build the network.

Actually, they had to build two networks. Where a lot of prior research on networks built models that lumped any and all types of connections together, these researchers needed to sort out the economic network from the social one. To do this, they found that it was easier to draw two models and then combine them, so they could find overlaps and sift out each type of connection from one big model. First, they asked the surveyed firms to list their suppliers over the past year. From there, they could draw a rough network based on purely economic transactions. Next, they asked firm leaders to tell them who in the industry they sought out for personal advice or guidance. From there, they could build a network based on social interactions. When they laid one network on top of the other, a picture of a truly multiplex network appeared.

This new network model allowed the researchers to estimate the extent to which the presence of one type of tie increases the probability of another tie being present. They found out it is surprisingly common. When two founders of two different firms shared either an economic or social tie, it was more likely than chance that they would develop the second tie. Perhaps more interestingly, the researchers found that if two founders of two different firms shared a social tie (they sought each other out for advice or considered each other friends), they were more than twice as likely to develop an economic tie (doing business together) than if they had shared an economic tie first and then later developed a social one. To put it another way, *it is more likely that personal will become business than it is that business will become personal*.

Multiplex ties, these findings indicate, are more likely to develop because friends begin to do more business together than the other way around. This supports the examples of Procter & Gamble and Ben & Jerry's. Both were companies started because an initial personal connection turned into a multiplex one when the two founders went into business together.

Taken together, these findings suggest that there are potential business opportunities and relationships to be had inside of what most of us would consider our friendship network. While we want to avoid taking an instrumental approach to all of our relationships—not judging the quality of a friendship by how well it serves our career or business interests—it is still worth considering how open we are to the idea that these self-developed categories of personal and business don't actually reflect the reality of our network. The Bologna study proves that personal can indeed become business.

But what about making business personal? Are multiplex relationships inside of the workplace, or between two individuals who have a business relationship, a worthwhile pursuit?

That was the question that Jessica Methot, now at Rutgers University, sought to answer. Methot, along with her colleagues Jeffery LePine, Nathan Podsakoff, and Jessica Siegel Christian, studied the development of multiplex relationships inside of companies to determine if they were helpful or harmful to performance.[13] In the first of two studies, the researchers surveyed 168 employees of an insurance company in the southeastern United States. The organization itself actually encouraged employees to get to know everyone else in the company by allowing them to temporarily shift positions horizontally in the organization and to work with different teams than their usual ones. The researchers asked all of the employees surveyed for the names of up to ten coworkers to whom they would go for assistance with job challenges (a work-related tie).

Then they asked the same employees to list the names of up to ten coworkers whom they considered to be friends (a personal tie). From there, just like the researchers in the Bologna study, Methot and her colleagues were able to turn the two lists into networks and the two networks into one multiplex picture of the organization. They also asked employees questions about emotional exhaustion and the work environment itself. Then, four to six weeks after the survey was completed, the researchers asked the employees' supervisors to fill out a performance appraisal.

Putting it all together, Methot and her colleagues (some of whom she'd probably label as friends) could examine the network of the organization and also see how that network affected performance, burnout, and how positive or negative the overall environment was. They found that multiplex relationships—having a lot of coworkers who eventually developed into friends—significantly increased employees' performance (as judged by their supervisor). But this came at a cost. Multiplex relationships also triggered a higher rate of emotional exhaustion—keeping up with more and deeper relationships can be tough. While the emotional toll itself decreased performance, the positive gains from having a coworker who was also a friend more than outweighed the negatives.

In a follow-up study, this one conducted across multiple companies in multiple industries, the researchers found a similar effect. Becoming friends with our coworkers might be a little more draining emotionally, but it makes us far more productive overall. "Workplace friends influence performance over and above purely instrumental or pure friendship-based relationships," the authors write.[14]

So friendship connections often become work connections, and at work, coworkers can become friends and everyone's performance is boosted. But does multiplexity—specifically, a mixing of business and personal relationships—benefit companies themselves, beyond the individual boosts in performance that Methot and colleagues found? It turns out that it does. Beyond productivity, multiplex connections also appear to enhance the innovation and knowledge-sharing inside of an organization.

Evidence for this comes from a trio of researchers in the Netherlands led by Rick Aalbers.[15] The team studied how formal and informal relationships in organizations, as well as multiplex relationships that are both formal and informal, can affect the sharing of innovative knowledge. While it has been well known for some time that every organization has both a formal network (the lines and boxes of the planned organizational chart) and an informal network (the actual personal relationships that are built, including across departments and functions), the researchers were investigating the role of multiplexity (a single relationship represented through both formal and informal ties) in how information was shared.

To do this, they studied two organizations in the Netherlands, one being an electronics and engineering subsidiary and the other a financial services provider. The researchers conducted interviews with various employees at both companies. As in similar studies, the researchers asked questions about friends (informal ties) and work colleagues (formal ties) and used that information to draw a rough set of network maps (formal, informal, and combined). They also asked questions related to conversations about new ideas, potential innovations, and product and process improvements (to measure knowledge-sharing and information). Lastly, they consulted a wealth of written materials like project plans, meeting minutes, and anything else that helped them better understand who was connected to whom.

Surprisingly, the researchers found that both the formal and informal networks somewhat explained the pathways taken by ideas and knowledge through the organization. But these networks didn't tell the whole story. Only when they also considered multiplex ties, those friends and informal contacts who also had a formal relationship, did the researchers get the most accurate picture of how good ideas spread. "Relations that combine formal as well as informal aspects into a single relation between two persons have a genuinely distant and significantly positive effect on innovative knowledge transfer within organizations," they wrote.[16] These "rich ties" are a huge benefit to organizations of all shapes and sizes.

Taken together, these studies are just a portion of the knowledge we've acquired about multiplex ties, but they are enough to push back against the notion that business and personal are two different categories. *Humans are humans, and the mechanisms behind their relationships don't seem to change depending on the setting.* Multiplex relationships—business that is also personal—help individuals make decisions about whom to do business with, help employees perform better because they have friends at work, and even help the broader organization take better advantage of good ideas. More than that, sometimes multiplex ties can create once-in-a-lifetime opportunities and shape an individual's entire career.

From Pianist to Venture Capitalist

When she first walked into the offices of Smith Barney to apply for the sales assistant job, a fancy title for what was essentially a secretary, no one would have seen Whitney Johnson as the future head of an influential investment firm.[17] But that is exactly what she became. She had graduated from college in her late twenties, and with a degree in music. She had never taken a finance or accounting course, but she was an accomplished pianist—those evaluating her application probably just figured that meant she could type fast. She was hired and expected to be a great assistant. But she quickly developed a desire to exceed that expectation. Rather than just assist the action, she wanted to be a part of it.

"I was lucky because I had a boss who was willing to promote me from assistant to the professional side," Johnson explained. "Which is really rare for the industry, and especially rare for a woman, but I was determined."[18] She started taking business and finance courses at night and proved her mettle to become a professional. She got the promotion, but she still wasn't done. In trying to grow her career and strive for the brass ring, she had a competitive advantage. She was fluent in Spanish, having spent over a year as a missionary in Uruguay, and she parlayed that skill (along with her newly learned finance and accounting skills) to become an investment analyst, studying media and telecom companies in Mexico and developing financial models and trend analysis for the institutional investors making high-stakes investment decisions. She was good at it. After just one year, she found herself ranked number three by *Institutional Investor* magazine, which surveys investors and ranks analysts on the quality of their information. After that she was ranked number one in her niche for eight years straight, except for one year. "I had a baby," Johnson joked.

But in achieving so much, Johnson also felt that she had hit a ceiling. There wasn't really a path that led higher. She realized this as she and her husband were moving from New York City to Boston so that he could accept a faculty position. She commuted back and forth to her work in New York, but after a while she found that it wasn't worth the effort anymore, so she left and started exploring other options. She wrote a children's book that didn't get published. She pitched a television show in Latin America that didn't get developed. She also started volunteering more. Johnson found herself on a committee at her church that sought to increase engagement between religious and business leaders. The head of the committee was a Harvard Business School professor named Clayton Christensen.

Christensen was renowned in the strategy and innovation world as the mind behind the theory of "disruptive innovation."[19] Put simply, innovative companies often start at the low end of the market, capturing customers that larger, entrenched companies don't find worthwhile. Fueled by success on the low end, eventually these innovators move up-market and overtake the entrenched companies (as Netflix did to Blockbuster, or Amazon did to Borders), and the result is disruptive innovation. Johnson had seen disruptive innovation play out when she was an investment analyst, and she was familiar with Christensen's work. She had even written to Christensen a few times to show how his theory explained the shifts in Latin America's telecommunications industry.

But in truth, she had not really established a relationship with him. Now, serving with him on a church committee, she developed a personal friendship with Christensen. Eventually the head of the committee, who had recruited Johnson to join, left, and Johnson became the head. In addition to growing their friendship, the committee gave Christensen a chance to see how Johnson worked firsthand.

"I got to know him. He got to know me," Johnson recalled. "He saw that I was capable and competent."[20] Over the course of working together for almost two years, Johnson also got to see what Christensen was working on. Alongside his son, who was about to graduate from business school, Christensen was beginning to apply the theory of disruptive innovation to investing. (Christensen had previously invested his money in Netflix and had also bet against Blockbuster in the market.) The pair had already received some positive feedback about how their theory guided investment decisions (including the cold emails from Johnson years before) and were investigating starting an investment firm. But Christensen didn't have experience in finance, and neither did his son. So they knew they needed a partner or two who could bring that knowledge to their operation.

Fortunately, Christensen was sitting across the committee table from such a person every week. As a professor at Harvard Business School, Christensen could have used his professional contacts to find several well-qualified financiers. He could have used his status as a professor to recruit a dozen high-energy MBAs. He could have mounted a nationwide search for a company president. Instead, like the entrepreneurs in the Bologna study, he chose to reach out to a personal connection and grow it into a professional one. He asked Johnson to join them as the third founder-partner of what would become Rose Park Advisors. They raised capital for their flagship "Disruptive Innovation Fund," and Johnson took on the role of president of the firm in 2007. Under her tenure, the fund brought its investors a rate of return almost ten times higher than the market average. While it's unknown how they would have fared had Christensen selected a different professional contact, it is safe to say that the whole team was grateful they took a chance on a personal connection and turned it into a multiplex relationship.

While founder friendships like Ben and Jerry's, or family partnerships like Procter & Gamble, or even friendships turned business connections like Bill Gates or Whitney Johnson, exist everywhere we look, we still have a tendency to separate business from personal. But actual human networks are much more complex and complicated than simple mental models imply. A significant portion of our relationships are multiplex, and significant opportunity lies in growing solo ties into multiplex ones. Whether it is business success that grows from personal connections or lifelong friendship that develops from working alongside each other, the return on relationships is great—as long as we are willing to invest and grow them into richer, deeper, multiplex ties.

FROM SCIENCE TO PRACTICE

Whether you are an entrepreneur, an employee, or a hopeful future employee, the research on multiplexity in social networks strikingly contradicts our typical assumptions about how connections are categorized. While we might separate our "business" contacts from our "personal" ones and think, "It's not personal, it's just business," personal relationships quite often become business (and vice versa). In addition, as with Whitney Johnson and Clayton Christensen, personal friendships can become long-lasting and valuable business relationships. If you have been thinking you need to maintain separation between your friends and your colleagues, then it's time to rethink your assumptions. Start by opening up your perspective about your friends and coworkers, and then start widening your relationships. Here's how:

1. List five friends who do work you know very little about.
2. Set a time to meet with each one in the next thirty days, for coffee or lunch or just to hang out. Make sure to take time to ask questions about what they are working on. You're not looking for anything specific that will help your own work or create an opportunity. You're just looking to learn. (These *are* your friends after all; you're not trying to take advantage of them.)
3. Make a list of five colleagues whom you don't know very well.
4. Make an appointment to meet with each one of your colleagues in the next thirty days. As with your friends, you're looking to learn. If you sense that they don't want to reveal too much about themselves, then don't worry. (They probably haven't read this chapter of this book yet.) But take an

interest in them and show it. You never know, you might make a new best friend.

Practicing Online

In the online world, social media websites often further the divide in our thinking between business and personal. There are services like LinkedIn for professional contacts and ones like Facebook and Instagram for personal ones. Some industries even have their own specialized social networks that work like LinkedIn and are just for academics, or creatives, or whoever else you can think of. If you are looking to grow colleagues into friends, or friends into coworkers, it may be helpful to start by determining whether you're connected with them on just one service or both—if not, then reach out. If they don't respond to your friend request, don't feel bad. Everyone has different rules of thumb for how they categorize relationships. But you've done a great deed just by demonstrating your openness.

For a downloadable template to use when completing this exercise, go to http://davidburkus.com/resources/ and look for networking resources.

Conclusion

Or
Why You Should Choose Each Friend of a Friend Carefully

IN THE LATE 1990S, Dr. Nicholas Christakis was troubled. As a physician working in hospice care, he was no stranger to death—he knew that his patients were close to death. What troubled him more and more was watching the toll that one death in a relationship took on the surviving member. Often when a married person fell terminally ill, he noticed, the spouse would quickly develop a life-threatening illness as well. As a researcher and medical doctor, Christakis was familiar with the "widowhood effect" and had even researched it. But he was beginning to wonder: if a marital relationship has such a strong effect on health, do other kinds of relationships have noticeable effects too?[1]

Christakis pondered this possibility as he transitioned from working in Chicago's South Side to conducting research at Harvard University in Cambridge. By then, he had decided he wanted to study the health effects of relationships—but he had also decided it was too big a task to research all on his own. In the true fashion of networks, a potential partner emerged through a friend of a friend. Christakis was introduced by a colleague to

James Fowler, who worked on campus with him (in an adjoining building in fact). Fowler was studying networks, mostly from a political perspective. Together, the two decided they wanted to take on the new challenge of looking at how our social networks affect our health—but doing so would require collecting massive amounts of data.

In fact, when Christakis and Fowler were outlining their project and looking for grants, their initial estimate was that it would cost around $25 million to collect and analyze the data needed to answer their question.[2] Needless to say, it was hard to find a donor. Undeterred, Christakis and Fowler began looking for preliminary data—data that had already been collected—with the hope that they might be able to use some of it as a proof of concept in their grant proposals. Instead, they stumbled upon an unexpected wealth of health and network data hidden in Framingham, Massachusetts.

Since 1948, researchers from Boston University have been following a community of people in Framingham. The researchers began a set of regular interviews and physical examinations with more than 5,000 men and women from the town. As the initial participants grew older, the researchers then enrolled a second and eventually a third generation of participants. While the amount of effort put into studying these residents has been immense, so have the findings that have resulted from the Framingham Heart Study. Much of what we know about heart disease can be traced back to this study.

When Christakis and Fowler examined the data, however, they found that it covered more than just the heart health of the participants. They were studied for all sorts of medical conditions, and during interviews they were probed with all sorts of demographic questions, including questions about family members and friends. In the end, the Framingham Heart Study researchers had collected so much information that Christakis and Fowler didn't end up needing a $25 million grant—they just needed to ask different questions of this already massive data set.

To start, Christakis and Fowler chose something relatively simple to measure objectively: obesity. Unlike a lot of health conditions that require that a patient first present with symptoms, obesity measurements generally rely on body-mass index (BMI), a measurement of your weight relative to your height. Since height and weight were taken at almost every physical examination, it was easy to see a progression over time. If someone was given a BMI of over 30, he or she was considered obese. The interview data, especially survey questions about family and friendships, allowed the pair to construct a network map of participants in the study; the fact that those questions were asked again during follow-up examinations allowed them to track changes in the network over time.

When they had constructed their evolving network map, including who had developed obesity and when, they found something amazing: obesity really was an epidemic.[3] Not only was it increasing in prevalence, but the spread of obesity seemed to be influenced by the network.

According to their results, if a friend of yours becomes obese, you yourself are 45 percent more likely than chance to gain weight over the next two to four years. More surprisingly, however, Christakis and Fowler found that if *a friend of your friend* becomes obese, your likelihood of gaining weight increases by about 20 percent—even if you don't know that friend of a friend. The effect continues one more person out. If a friend of the friend of your friend develops obesity, you are still 10 percent more likely than random chance to gain weight as well. Moreover, their results suggest that more is going on than a tendency among obese people to hang out together. Because they surveyed people over thirty-two years, they were able to show a real cause-and-effect relationship between individual friends (and friends of friends) and weight gains. While the researchers looked for a variety of explanations, the most likely one appears to be norms. If your friend is obese or a friend of a friend is obese, that changes your perception of what is an acceptable body size and your behavior changes accordingly.

When Christakis and Fowler's results were published in the *New England Journal of Medicine,* the reaction was predictably strong. The story that "your friends might be making you fat" was quickly and enthusiastically covered by major media outlets. That finding certainly made for a sensational headline, but the more intriguing finding of Christakis and Fowler's original study is not that weight gain is an epidemic, but rather that we are subtly influenced by people we likely don't even know. The researchers termed this effect "three degrees of influence." While we might be separated from everyone in the world by six or fewer degrees, three of those six degrees appear to be influencing us in ways we are not even aware of.

In a follow-up study, Christakis and Fowler found something similar with smoking rates.[4] Using the same social network data they had borrowed from the Framingham Heart Study, they studied smoking rates and, in particular, the decline of smoking over the length of the study. From the time the Framingham study began until the modern day, smoking declined gradually—in a way that has been the reverse of the obesity epidemic (which unfortunately might lend validity to the commonly held belief that smoking helps people lose weight).

The initial results for the effect of three degrees of influence on smoking showed it to be even greater than for obesity. If your friend smokes, the researchers found, you are 61 percent more likely to be a smoker yourself. If a friend of your friend smokes, you are still 29 percent more likely to smoke. And for a friend of that friend, the likelihood is 11 percent. The researchers could also see how, over time, quitting smoking increases the chances that others in your network will also stop. "When one person quits smoking, it has a ripple effect on his friends, his friends' friends, and his friends' friends' friends," they wrote of their results. "There is a kind of synchrony in time and space when it comes to smoking cessation that resembles the flocking of birds or schooling of fish."[5]

And it wasn't just physical health affected by three degrees of influence. Christakis and Fowler also found this effect holding for our moods and mental health.[6] Returning to the Framingham Heart Study participants, the pair found that examiners had asked participants a series of questions taken from the Center of Epidemiological Studies Depression Scale. Four of the twenty items to which participants respond on the CES-D have been shown in prior studies to correlate well with measurements of happiness. The questions ask each respondent how often in the past week he or she "felt hopeful," "was happy," "enjoyed life," and felt that he or she was "just as good as other people." Using these four questions, Christakis and Fowler could track how happy and unhappy people clustered together, and also how other people's happiness might affect a participant's own happiness. They found that participants were about 15 percent more likely to be happy if they were connected to another happy person. In addition, they were around 10 percent more likely to be happy if a friend of their connection was happy. For friends of friends of friends, the likelihood was nearly 6 percent.

While an increase in happiness of 6 percent from someone three degrees away being happy may not seem like all that much, Christakis and Fowler are quick to point out that studies suggest that an increase in income of around $10,000 has a 2 percent chance of increasing happiness. "So, having happy friends and relatives appears to be a more effective predictor of happiness than earning more money," they wrote.[7] Since the "hat-trick" of their findings about social networks and the spread of influence, additional published research has supported their findings, in domains as diverse as political beliefs, innovative ideas, financial panic, and even suicide.

Throughout this book, we've examined how social networks operate and how they create opportunities in work and in life. We've seen how weak ties and degrees of separation keep you more connected than you might think. We've seen how some individuals can navigate a collection of relationships far larger than you may imagine to be manageable, and also how you can dramatically grow the number of your own connections (or appear to already have a dramatic number of connections). We've discovered that the relationships among silos, clusters, and new and unlikely connections are more nuanced and complex than many people assume. And we've seen how we tend to be drawn to areas of the larger network that we're more comfortable and familiar with, even when making connections in those areas is not necessarily in our best interest. Now the findings from Christakis and Fowler and all of the researchers they influenced offer us one final lesson—and perhaps the most important one.

Social networks certainly have value because of the potential connections they can unlock, but they also have value because of their influence on ourselves. More than just influencing the people around you to help you gain social capital, social networks enable the people around you to influence you in positive and negative ways we're only now becoming aware of. You aren't just influenced by your friends and by friends of friends. Who you have become as a person, in whatever career you have chosen, was influenced by the network around you—and around your friends, and around friends of your friends—most likely without you even being aware of it.

We don't *have* a network; rather, we're *embedded inside* a massive network that we must learn to navigate. Doing so requires paying attention to who is in your network and recognizing that how your network works matters for issues much larger than just finding that next client or landing that next job. Social networks aren't just transactional, and they never were. They're developmental. Your network is influencing you, and so you better begin influencing your network. Navigating your network deliberately—making choices about *who* your friends are and being aware of who is a friend of a friend—can directly influence the person you become, for better or worse.

Your friend of a friend is your future.

Going Further

For further study of the science of networks and best practices when building and strengthening connections, I have created a collection of extra resources, including full-length interviews with several people profiled in this book, videos, and recommended readings. In addition, I've compiled a workbook of the exercises outlined at the end of each chapter. Because of the changing nature of technology, I will continue to keep these resources updated on my website with the most valuable and relevant information.

All of these resources are freely available at my website, http://www.davidburkus.com/resources.

Acknowledgments

Every good book requires a good team, and every good team requires a good network. It's your decision as to whether or not this was a good book, but I can tell you that the people who shaped it were a great team. I am fortunate in that I have had the chance to meet, and work with, so many great people in writing *Friend of a Friend:*

Rick Wolff, my editor, who caught the idea quickly and helped shape it into reality, as well as Rosemary McGuinness, Lisa Glover, Cindy Buck, Taryn Roeder, Bruce Nichols, and everyone at Houghton Mifflin Harcourt.

Giles Anderson, my agent, who regularly talks me out of the bad ideas and into great ones.

Tom Neilssen, Les Tuerk, Cynthia Seeto, Adam Kirschenbaum, and all the folks at BrightSight Group for their help in finding a stage (or stages) for these ideas.

Several great minds who assisted me with amazing insights and who helped me—and continue to help me—spread the word about *Friend of a Friend:* Tim Grahl, Jeff Goins, Ryan Holiday, Becky Robinson, Ashley Bernardi, and Tracey Lucas.

The amazing people with amazing stories who made themselves available to me for interviews: Andrew Davis, Jon Levy, Chris Schembra, Whitney Johnson, Jayson Gaignard, Jordan Harbinger, Brian Uzzi, and Scott Harrison.

The fascinating minds who helped me shape the stories and

ideas in this book: Tom Webster, Tamsen Webster, Mitch Joel, Clay Hebert, and Bret Simmons.

Two amazing clusters I found myself in during the writing of this book—private groups of business authors who became such a valuable resource that C. S. Lewis and Ernest Hemingway would be jealous. You know who you are.

My research assistants Brendan Campagna and Will Cook, who made this project easier, but not as easy as Reagan Kingsley made it thanks to his tireless photocopying.

My chief of staff, Neha Ghelani, who kept telling me what to stop doing so that I could find the time to do this.

The faculty and staff of Oral Roberts University, particularly the College of Business and Dr. Rebecca Gunn, who probably proofread this manuscript more than I did.

And my wife Janna and boys Lincoln and Harrison, the most important friends that I know.

Notes

Introduction

1. Adam Grant, *Give and Take: Why Helping Others Drives Our Success* (New York: Viking, 2013).
2. Ibid., 48.
3. Ibid.
4. Jessica Shambora, "Fortune's Best Networker," *Fortune*, February 9, 2011.
5. Adam Rifkin, "Networking for Success," *Startups.co*, https://www.startups.co/education/lessons/networking-for-success.
6. Adam Rifkin, "The Basics of Power Networking," *LinkedIn*, August 6, 2013, https://www.linkedin.com/pulse/20130806141819-8244-3-important-things-to-be-mindful-of-as-you-build-your-network.
7. Rifkin, "Networking for Success."
8. Ibid.
9. "All advice is autobiographical" has been attributed to many people, but it's most often attributed to Austin Kleon, *Steal Like an Artist: 10 Things Nobody Told You About Being Creative* (New York: Workman, 2012), 1.
10. Tiziana Casciaro, Francesca Gino, and Maryam Kouchaki, "The Contaminating Effects of Building Instrumental Ties: How Networking Can Make Us Feel Dirty," *Administrative Science Quarterly* 59, no. 4 (2014): 705–735.
11. George P. Bush and Lowell H. Hattery, "Federal Recruitment of Junior Engineers," *Science* 114, no. 2966 (1951): 455–458.
12. Rob Cross and Robert J. Thomas, "Managing Yourself: A Smarter Way to Network," *Harvard Business Review* 89 (2011): 149–153.
13. Robert D. Putnam, *Bowling Alone: The Collapse and Revival of American Community* (New York: Simon & Schuster, 2000).
14. Ronald S. Burt and Don Ronchi, "Teaching Executives to See Social Capital: Results from a Field Experiment," *Social Science Research* 36 (2007): 1156–1183.
15. Brian A. Primack, Ariel Shensa, Jaime E. Sidani, Erin O. Whaite, Liu yi Lin, Daniel Rosen, Jason B. Colditz, Ana Radovic, and Elizabeth Miller, "Social Media Use and Perceived Social Isolation Among Young Adults in the US," *American Journal of Preventive Medicine* 53, no. 1 (2017): 1–8.

1. Find Strength in Weak Ties

1. Shane Rivers, "The Life of Lorenzo Fertitta," *Gaming the Odds,* February 15, 2015, http://www.gamingtheodds.com/biographies/lorenzo-fertitta.
2. Case Keefer, "Lorenzo Fertitta, Dana White Built UFC into Something Big," *Las Vegas Sun,* June 29, 2014.
3. Joel Stein, "The Ultimate Fighting Machines," *CNN Money,* November 8, 2006, http://money.cnn.com/2006/11/07/magazines/business2/stationcasinos.biz2/.
4. Matthew G. Miller, "Fertittas Made Billionaires by Head Blows with Chokeholds," *Bloomberg,* August 1, 2012, https://www.bloomberg.com/news/articles/2012-08-01/fertittas-made-billionaires-by-head-blows-with-chokeholds.
5. Stein, "The Ultimate Fighting Machines."
6. Ibid.
7. Rivers, "The Life of Lorenzo Fertitta."
8. Miller, "Fertittas Made Billionaires by Head Blows with Chokeholds."
9. Jeff Haden, "The UFC Sells for $4 Billion: Partners Were Legally Bound to Settle Disputes by Actually Fighting," *Inc.,* July 11, 2016, http://www.inc.com/jeff-haden/ufc-sells-for-4b-partners-were-legally-bound-to-settle-disputes-by-actually-figh.html.
10. Ibid.
11. Keefer, "Lorenzo Fertitta, Dana White Built UFC into Something Big."
12. Rivers, "The Life of Lorenzo Fertitta."
13. Ibid.
14. "Lorenzo Fertitta Touts UFC Sale as 'Largest Deal Ever in the History of Sports,'" *Fox Sports,* July 11, 2016, http://www.foxsports.com/ufc/story/ufc-lorenzo-fertitta-touts-ufc-sale-as-largest-deal-ever-in-the-history-of-sports-071116.
15. Nicole Laporte, "Why WME-IMG Paid $4 Billion for UFC, a Mixed Martial Arts League," *Fast Company,* July 11, 2016, https://www.fastcompany.com/3061739/why-wme-img-paid-4-billion-for-ufc-a-mixed-martial-arts-league.
16. Jason Gay, "Dana White Continues the Fight," *Wall Street Journal,* February 12, 2017.
17. Mark S. Granovetter, "The Strength of Weak Ties," *American Journal of Sociology* 78, no. 6 (1973): 1360–1380.
18. Ibid., 1371.
19. Martin Ruef, "Strong Ties, Weak Ties, and Islands: Structural and Cultural Predictors of Organizational Innovation," *Industrial and Corporate Change* 11, no. 3 (2002): 427–449.
20. Mary Petrusewicz, "Note to Entrepreneurs: Meet New People," *Stanford Report,* January 21, 2004, http://news.stanford.edu/news/2004/january21/innovate-121.html.
21. Ruef, "Strong Ties, Weak Ties, and Islands," 445.
22. Granovetter, "The Strength of Weak Ties," 1372.

23. Daniel Z. Levin, Jorge Walter, and J. Keith Murnighan, "Dormant Ties: The Value of Reconnecting," *Organization Science* 22, no. 4 (2011): 923–939.
24. Daniel Z. Levin, Jorge Walter, and J. Keith Murnighan, "The Power of *Reconnection:* How Dormant Ties Can Surprise You," *MIT Sloan Management Review* (Spring 2011), http://sloanreview.mit.edu/article/the-power-of-reconnection-how-dormant-ties-can-surprise-you/.
25. Ibid.
26. Jorge Walter, Daniel Z. Levin, and J. Keith Murnighan, "Reconnection Choices: Selecting the Most Valuable (vs. Most Preferred) Dormant Ties," *Organization Science* 26, no. 5 (2015): 1447–1465.
27. Jorge Walter, Daniel Z. Levin, and J. Keith Murnighan, "How to Reconnect for Maximum Impact," *MIT Sloan Management Review* (Spring 2016), http://sloanreview.mit.edu/article/how-to-reconnect-for-maximum-impact/.
28. Andrew Warner, "How charity: water Is Using Social Media to Save the World" (podcast), *Mixergy,* July 21, 2010, https://mixergy.com/interviews/charity-water-scott-harrison-interview/.
29. charity: water, "Scott's Story," http://www.charitywater.org/about/scotts_story.php.
30. Ibid.
31. Warner, "How charity: water Is Using Social Media to Save the World."
32. Ibid.
33. David Baker, "Charity Startup: Scott Harrison's Mission to Solve Africa's Water Problem," *Wired,* January 4, 2013, http://www.wired.co.uk/article/charity startup.
34. Scott Harrison, interview with the author, April 11, 2017.
35. Ibid.
36. Baker, "Charity Startup: Scott Harrison's Mission to Solve Africa's Water Problem."
37. Warner, "How charity: water Is Using Social Media to Save the World."
38. Ibid.
39. Ibid.
40. Scott Harrison, interview with the author, April 11, 2017.
41. Warner, "How charity: water Is Using Social Media to Save the World."

2. See Your Whole Network

1. Steven H. Strogatz, *Sync: How Order Emerges from Chaos in the Universe, Nature, and Daily Life* (New York: Hachette, 2003).
2. For "the most comprehensive version of the Kevin Bacon game on the web," see the Oracle of Kevin Bacon website at: https://oracleofbacon.org.
3. Craig Fass, Brian Turtle, and Mike Ginelli, *Six Degrees of Kevin Bacon* (New York City: Plume, 1996), 15.

4. Strogatz, *Sync: How Order Emerges from Chaos in the Universe, Nature, and Daily Life*.
5. John Boitnott, "How Kevin Bacon Is Solving One of the Biggest Problems with Celebrities and Charities," *Inc.*, January 31, 2017, http://www.inc.com/john-boitnott/how-kevin-bacon-is-solving-one-of-the-biggest-problems-with-celebrities-and-char.html.
6. David Burkus, *The Myths of Creativity: The Truth About How Innovative Companies and People Generate Great Ideas* (San Francisco: Jossey-Bass, 2013).
7. American Mathematical Society, "Collaboration Distance," http://www.ams.org/mathscinet/freeTools.html.
8. Stanley Milgram, "Behavioral Study of Obedience," *Journal of Abnormal and Social Psychology* 67, no. 4 (1963): 371–378.
9. Brian Uzzi, "Keys to Understanding Your Social Capital," *Journal of Microfinance/ESR Review* 10 (2008): 7.
10. Jeffrey Travers and Stanley Milgram, "An Experimental Study of the Small World Problem," *Sociometry* 32, no. 4 (1969): 425–443.
11. Milgram also ran a similar experiment with participants in Wichita, Kansas. However, the results of that study were not included in his peer-reviewed article and so have been left out here.
12. Stanley Milgram, "The Small-World Problem," *Psychology Today* 2 (1969): 60–67.
13. Mark E. J. Newman, *Networks: An Introduction* (Oxford: Oxford University Press, 2010).
14. Albert-László Barabási, *Linked: How Everything Is Connected to Everything Else and What It Means for Business, Science, and Everyday Life* (New York: Basic Books, 2014).
15. Travers and Milgram, "An Experimental Study of the Small World Problem."
16. Milgram, "The Small-World Problem."
17. Mark Buchanan, *Nexus: Small Worlds and the Groundbreaking Science of Networks* (New York: W. W. Norton and Co., 2002).
18. Duncan J. Watts and Steven H. Strogatz, "Collective Dynamics of 'Small-World' Networks," *Nature* 393 (1993): 440–442.
19. "Rod Steiger," *Internet Movie Database*, http://www.imdb.com/name/nm0001768/.
20. Strogatz, *Sync: How Order Emerges from Chaos in the Universe, Nature, and Daily Life*.
21. Peter Sheridan Dodds, Roby Muhamad, and Duncan J. Watts, "An Experimental Study of Search in Global Search Networks," *Science* 301, no. 5634 (2003): 827–829.
22. Duncan J. Watts, *Everything Is Obvious*: *Once You Know the Answer* (New York: Crown Business, 2011), 89.
23. Smriti Bhagat, Moira Burke, Carlos Diuk, Ismail Onur Filiz, and Sergey Edu-

nov, "Three and a Half Degrees of Separation," *Facebook Research*, February 4, 2016, https://research.fb.com/three-and-a-half-degrees-of-separation/.

24. Barabási, *Linked: How Everything Is Connected to Everything Else and What It Means for Business, Science, and Everyday Life*, 29.
25. John Guare, *Six Degrees of Separation: A Play* (New York: Dramatists Play Service, 1992), 79.
26. Whitney Johnson, "Episode 01: Michelle McKenna-Doyle" (audio podcast), *Disrupt Yourself Podcast*, September 21, 2016, https://itunes.apple.com/us/podcast/disrupt-yourself-podcast-whitney/id1156483471.
27. Ibid.
28. Ibid.
29. Auburn University, "Take 5: Michelle McKenna-Doyle," November 17, 2014, http://www.auburn.edu/main/take5/mckenna-doyle.html#.WMmaQRiVS9Y.
30. Johnson, "Episode 01: Michelle McKenna-Doyle."

3. Become a Broker and Fill Structural Holes

1. Bruce Feiler, "She's Playing Games with Your Lives," *New York Times*, April 27, 2012.
2. Jane McGonigal, *SuperBetter: The Power of Living Gamefully* (New York: Penguin, 2016), 3.
3. Ibid.
4. Scott Barry Kaufman, "Jane McGonigal on How Video Games Can Make Us SuperBetter" (audio podcast), *Psychology Podcast*, October 11, 2015, http://scottbarrykaufman.com/podcast/jane-mcgonigal-on-how-video-games-can-make-us-superbetter/.
5. Feiler, "She's Playing Games with Your Lives."
6. Jane McGonigal, email message to the author, April 17, 2017.
7. McGonigal, *SuperBetter*, 4.
8. Kaufman, "Jane McGonigal on How Video Games Can Make Us SuperBetter."
9. Ibid.
10. Ibid.
11. Jane McGonigal, email message to the author, April 17, 2017.
12. Ronald S. Burt, *Structural Holes: The Social Structure of Competition* (Cambridge, MA: Harvard University Press, 1995), 19.
13. Ibid., 18.
14. Ronald S. Burt, "Structural Holes and Good Ideas," *American Journal of Sociology* 110 (2004): 356.
15. Frans Johansson, *The Medici Effect: What Elephants and Epidemics Can Teach Us About Innovation* (Boston: Harvard Business School Publishing, 2017).
16. Cherokee Nation, "History of Sequoyah, and the Sequoyan Syllabary for the Cherokee Language," http://www.cherokee.org/About-The-Nation/History/Biographies/Sequoyah.

17. Burt, "Structural Holes and Good Ideas," 376.
18. Ibid., 349.
19. Adam M. Kleinbaum, "Organizational Misfits and the Origins of Brokerage in Intrafirm Networks," *Administrative Science Quarterly* 57 (2012): 407–452.
20. Ibid., 429.
21. Stanley A. McChrystal, David Silverman, Chris Fussell, and Tantum Collins, *Team of Teams: New Rules of Engagement for a Complex World* (New York: Portfolio, 2015), 118. General McChrystal cowrote *Team of Teams* with multiple authors, who chose to write the book in his voice. As such, I attribute quotes from this book to him.
22. Ibid., 118.
23. Ibid., 121.
24. Ibid., 122.
25. Ibid., 123.
26. Ibid., 128, 129.
27. Ibid., 128.
28. Ibid., 180.
29. Ibid., 251.
30. This activity was adapted from an exercise commonly described by the sociologist Brian Uzzi.

4. Seek Out Silos

1. Steven Johnson, *How We Got to Now: Six Innovations That Made the Modern World* (New York: Riverhead, 2014).
2. McChrystal et al., *Team of Teams: New Rules of Engagement for a Complex World,* 189–193.
3. Clifford Atiyeh, "GM Ignition-Switch Review Complete: 124 Fatalities, 274 Injuries," *Car and Driver,* August 3, 2015, http://blog.caranddriver.com/gm-ignition-switch-review-complete-124-fatalities-274-injuries/.
4. Eun Kyung Kim, "GM Chief Mary Barra on Car Recalls: 'I Don't Really Think There Was a Cover-up,'" *Today,* June 26, 2014, http://www.today.com/news/gm-chief-mary-barra-car-recalls-i-dont-really-think-1D79852194.
5. David Johnston, "9/11 Congressional Report Faults FBI-CIA Lapses," *New York Times,* July 24, 2003.
6. Michael Reynolds, *Hemingway: The Paris Years* (New York: W. W. Norton & Co., 1989).
7. David Burkus, "How Your Friends Affect Your Creative Work," *99U,* http://99u.com/articles/21521/in-praise-of-the-creative-support-group.
8. Charles Kadushin, *Understanding Social Networks: Theories, Concepts, and Findings* (Oxford: Oxford University Press, 2012), 122.
9. Mark E. J. Newman and Juyong Park, "Why Social Networks Are Different

from Other Types of Networks," *Physical Review E: Statistical, Linear, and Soft Matter Physics* 68, no. 3 (2003): 036122.

10. Damon Centola, "The Social Origin of Networks and Diffusion," *American Journal of Sociology* 120, no. 5 (2015): 1295–1338.
11. University of Pennsylvania, "In Social Networks, Group Boundaries Promote the Spread of Ideas, Study Finds," *ScienceDaily*, June 22, 2015, https://www.sciencedaily.com/releases/2015/06/150622182032.htm.
12. Ronald Burt and Jennifer Merluzzi, "Network Oscillation," *Academy of Management Discoveries* 2, no. 4 (2016): 368–391.
13. David Jon Phillips, "Networking Differently Could Increase Your Salary," *Chicago Booth Review*, September 1, 2016, http://review.chicagobooth.edu/strategy/2016/article/networking-differently-could-increase-your-salary.
14. Brian Uzzi, "Social Structure and Competition in Interfirm Networks: The Paradox of Embeddedness," *Administrative Science Quarterly* 42 (1997): 35–67.
15. Jeff Rosenthal, "How and Why to Curate Community," in Jared Kleinert, ed., *3 Billion Under 30: How Millennials Keep Redefining Success, Breaking Barriers, and Changing the World* (New York: 3 Billion Under 30 LLC, 2017).
16. Cathy Leff, "At Their Peak," *Cultured*, November 30, 2016, http://www.culturedmag.com/summit-series-jeff-rosenthal/.
17. Steven Bertoni, "Club TED: Inside Summit's Power Mountain Entrepreneur Camp," *Forbes*, January 21, 2013.
18. Andy Isaacson, "Summit Series: TED Meets Burning Man," *Wired*, February 27, 2012, https://www.wired.com/2012/02/summit-series-ted-burning-man/.
19. Andy Isaacson, "The Ski Resort That Crowdsourcing Built," *New York Times*, April 10, 2015.
20. J. Kelly Hoey, *Build Your Dream Network: Forging Powerful Relationships in a Hyper-Connected World* (New York: Tarcher/Perigee, 2017).
21. Alissa Walker, "TED for Design Wonks: CreativeMornings Offers Coffee and a Shot of Inspiration," *Wired*, June 11, 2012, https://www.wired.com/2012/06/creativemornings-conferences/.
22. Shutterstock, "Introducing Creative Mornings: An Interview with Tina Roth Eisenberg," December 4, 2013, https://vimeo.com/81051786.
23. Walker, "TED for Design Wonks: CreativeMornings Offers Coffee and a Shot of Inspiration."

5. Build Teams from All Over Your Network

1. Miguel Helft, "It Pays to Have Pals in Silicon Valley," *New York Times*, October 17, 2006.
2. "YouTube: A History," *The Telegraph*, April 17, 2010, http://www.telegraph.co.uk/finance/newsbysector/mediatechnologyandtelecoms/digital-media/7596636/YouTube-a-history.html.

3. Ibid.
4. "Youtube.com Traffic Statistics," *Alexa*, http://www.alexa.com/siteinfo/youtube.com (accessed March 16, 2017).
5. Conner Forrest, "How the 'PayPal Mafia' Redefined Success in Silicon Valley," *TechRepublic*, http://www.techrepublic.com/article/how-the-paypal-mafia-redefined-success-in-silicon-valley/.
6. Jeffrey M. O'Brien, "The PayPal Mafia," *Fortune*, November 13, 2007.
7. Forrest, "How the 'PayPal Mafia' Redefined Success in Silicon Valley."
8. O'Brien, "The PayPal Mafia."
9. Forrest, "How the 'PayPal Mafia' Redefined Success in Silicon Valley."
10. Rachel Rosmarin, "The PayPal Exodus," *Forbes*, July 12, 2006.
11. Forrest, "How the 'PayPal Mafia' Redefined Success in Silicon Valley."
12. Reid Hoffman and Ben Casnocha, *The Start-up of You: Adapt to the Future, Invest in Yourself, and Transform Your Career* (New York: Crown Business, 2012).
13. Shane Snow, *Smartcuts: How Hackers, Innovators, and Icons Accelerate Success* (New York: HarperCollins, 2014), 183.
14. Forrest, "How the 'PayPal Mafia' Redefined Success in Silicon Valley."
15. Stefan Wuchty, Benjamin F. Jones, and Brian Uzzi, "The Increasing Dominance of Teams in Production of Knowledge," *Science* 316, no. 5827 (2007): 1036–1039.
16. Roger Guimerà, Brian Uzzi, Jarrett Spiro, and Luís A. Nunes Amaral, "Team Assembly Mechanisms Determine Collaboration Network Structure and Team Performance," *Science* 308, no. 5722 (2005): 697–702.
17. Burkus, *The Myths of Creativity: The Truth About How Innovative Companies and People Generate Great Ideas*, 116.
18. Stefan H. Thomke and Ashok Nimgade, "IDEO Product Development," Case 600-143 (Boston: Harvard Business School, June 2000, revised April 2007).
19. Duane Bray, "IDEO's Employee Engagement Formula," *Harvard Business Review*, December 18, 2015, https://hbr.org/2015/12/ideos-employee-engagement-formula.
20. Ibid.
21. Jimmy Chion, "What It's Like to Work at IDEO," *Medium*, October 21, 2013, https://medium.com/@jimmmy/what-its-like-to-work-at-ideo-6ca2c961aae4#.89mbot8fh.
22. Teresa M. Amabile and Katrina Flanagan, "Making Progress at IDEO," Case 814-123 (Boston: Harvard Business School, June 2014), 5.
23. Margaret Schweer, Dimitris Assimakopoulos, Rob Cross, and Robert J. Thomas, "Building a Well-Networked Organization," *MIT Sloan Management Review* 53, no. 2 (2012): 35.

6. Become a Super-Connector

1. Brian Grazer and Charles Fishman, *A Curious Mind: The Secret to a Bigger Life* (New York: Simon & Schuster, 2016), 1–2.

2. Ibid., 2.
3. Ibid.
4. "Malcolm Gladwell with Brian Grazer: 92Y Talks: Episode 45" (audio podcast), 92Y *on Demand,* June 18, 2015, http://92yondemand.org/malcolm-gladwell-with-brian-grazer-92y-talks-episode-45.
5. Grazer and Fishman, *A Curious Mind: The Secret to a Bigger Life,* 4.
6. Ibid., 21.
7. Ibid.
8. Ibid., 51.
9. Ibid., 30.
10. Ibid.
11. Ibid., 231–258.
12. "Malcolm Gladwell with Brian Grazer: 92Y Talks Episode 45."
13. Robin I. M. Dunbar, "Coevolution of Neocortical Size, Group Size, and Language in Humans," *Behavioral and Brain Sciences* 16, no. 4 (1993): 681–694.
14. Russell Hill and Robin I. M. Dunbar, "Social Network Size in Humans," *Human Nature* 14, no. 1 (2003): 54.
15. Hans L. Zetterberg, *The Many-Splendored Society,* vol. 2, *A Language-Based Edifice of Social Structures* (zetterberg.org, 2011), http://zetterberg.org/InProgrs/The_Many-Splendored_Society/PDF_filer/VolumeTwoRefile2_20110516_2ndEd.pdf.
16. Tyler H. McCormick, Matthew J. Salganik, and Tian Zheng, "How Many People Do You Know? Efficiently Estimating Personal Network Size," *Journal of the American Statistical Association* 105, no. 489 (2010): 59–70.
17. Albert-László Barabási and Réka Albert, "Emergence of Scaling in Random Networks," *Science* 286, no. 5439 (1999): 509–512.
18. Jordan Harbinger, interview with the author, January 25, 2017.
19. Ibid.
20. Ibid.
21. Ibid.
22. Ibid.
23. Ibid.
24. Ibid.
25. Ibid.

7. Leverage Preferential Attachment

1. Jayson Gaignard, interview with the author, January 24, 2017.
2. Ibid.
3. Ibid.
4. Ibid.
5. Ibid.

6. Ibid.
7. Ibid.
8. Ibid.
9. Matthew 25:29 (NRSV).
10. Robert K. Merton, "The Matthew Effect in Science," *Science* 159, no. 3810 (1968): 56–63.
11. Barabási, *Linked: How Everything Is Connected to Everything Else and What It Means for Business, Science, and Everyday Life*, 87.
12. Barabási and Albert, "Emergence of Scaling in Random Networks."
13. Barabási, *Linked: How Everything Is Connected to Everything Else and What It Means for Business, Science, and Everyday Life*, 87.
14. Mark E. J. Newman, "Clustering and Preferential Attachment in Growing Networks," *Physical Review E: Statistical, Nonlinear, and Soft Matter Physics* 64, no. 211 (2001): 251021–251024.
15. Matthew J. Salganik, Peter Sheridan Dodds, and Duncan J. Watts, "Experimental Study of Inequality and Unpredictability in an Artificial Cultural Market," *Science* 311, no. 5762 (2006): 854–856.
16. Watts, *Everything Is Obvious*: *Once You Know the Answer*.
17. James Zug, "Stolen: How the Mona Lisa Became the World's Most Famous Painting," *Smithsonian.com*, June 15, 2011, http://www.smithsonianmag.com/arts-culture/stolen-how-the-mona-lisa-became-the-worlds-most-famous-painting-16406234/.
18. Watts, *Everything Is Obvious*: *Once You Know the Answer*.
19. Zug, "Stolen: How the Mona Lisa Became the World's Most Famous Painting."
20. Watts, *Everything Is Obvious*: *Once You Know the Answer*.
21. Zug, "Stolen: How the Mona Lisa Became the World's Most Famous Painting."
22. Watts, *Everything Is Obvious*: *Once You Know the Answer*. Duchamp was also an American citizen.

8. Create the Illusion of Majority

1. Tim Ferriss, "Introduction—My Story," http://tim.blog/introduction/.
2. Tim Ferriss, "A Lesson in Self Promotion with Tim Ferriss," *ZURB Soapbox*, http://zurb.com/soapbox/events/3/Tim-Ferriss-ZURBsoapbox.
3. Ibid.
4. Ibid.
5. Andrew Davis, interview with the author, January 9, 2017.
6. Ibid.
7. Ibid.
8. Ibid.
9. Ibid.
10. Ibid.

11. Ibid.
12. Ibid.
13. Scott L. Feld, "Why Your Friends Have More Friends Than You Do," *American Journal of Sociology* 96, no. 6 (1991): 1464–1477.
14. Naghmeh Momeni and Michael Rabbat, "Qualities and Inequalities in Online Social Networks Through the Lens of the Generalized Friendship Paradox," *PLoS ONE* 11, no. 2 (2016): e0143633.
15. Kristina Lerman, Xiaoran Yan, and Xin-Zeng Wu, "The 'Majority Illusion' in Social Networks," *PloS ONE* 11, no. 2 (2016): e0147617.
16. Ibid.
17. David Kirkpatrick, *The Facebook Effect: The Inside Story of the Company That Is Connecting the World* (New York: Simon & Schuster, 2001).
18. William Barnett and Arar Han, "Facebook 2012," Case E468 (Palo Alto, CA: Stanford Graduate School of Business Publishing, 2012).
19. William Barnett, Ziad Mokhtar, and Gabriel Tavridis, "Facebook," Case E220 (Palo Alto, CA: Stanford Graduate School of Business Publishing, 2006).
20. Kirkpatrick, *The Facebook Effect: The Inside Story of the Company That Is Connecting the World.*

9. Resist Homophily

1. Ryan W. Miller, "'The New York Times' Data Blog Flips Prediction in Two Hours," *USA Today,* November 8, 2016.
2. Nate Silver, "2016 Election Results: Live Coverage and Results," *FiveThirtyEight,* November 8, 2016, http://livethirtyeight.com/live-blog/2016-election-results-coverage/.
3. Ibid.
4. "Who Will Win the Presidency?" *FiveThirtyEight,* November 8, 2016, https://projects.fivethirtyeight.com/2016-election-forecast/.
5. Silver, "2016 Election Results: Live Coverage and Results."
6. Ibid.
7. Andreas Graefe, "A Terrible Day for Election Forecasters. Where Are the Winners?" *PollyVote,* November 9, 2016, http://pollyvote.com/en/2016/11/09/a-terrible-day-for-election-forecasters-where-are-the-winners/.
8. "They're with Her: PR Execs Predict a Resounding Clinton Victory," *PRWeek,* November 8, 2016, http://www.prweek.com/article/1414851/theyre-her-pr-execs-predict-resounding-clinton-victory.
9. Alec MacGillis, "Go Midwest, Young Hipster," *New York Times,* October 22, 2016.
10. Deepak Malhotra, "How to Build an Exit Ramp for Trump Supporters," *Harvard Business Review,* October 14, 2016, https://hbr.org/2016/10/how-to-build-an-exit-ramp-for-trump-supporters.

11. Jessie Hellmann, "Pelosi: Trump Will Help Democrats Win Congress," *The Hill*, June 19, 2016, http://thehill.com/blogs/ballot-box/presidential-races/284013-pelosi-trump-will-help-democrats-win-congress.
12. Amy Chozick, "Hillary Clinton Blames FBI Director for Election Loss," *New York Times*, November 12, 2016.
13. Joshua Spodek, "If You Voted for Trump, Let's Meet," *Inc.*, November 30, 2016, http://www.inc.com/joshua-spodek/if-you-voted-for-trump-lets-meet.html.
14. Edward-Isaac Dovere, "How Clinton Lost Michigan—and Blew the Election," *Politico*, December 14, 2016, http://www.politico.com/story/2016/12/michigan-hillary-clinton-trump-232547.
15. Glenn Thrush, "10 Crucial Decisions That Reshaped America," *Politico*, December 9, 2016, http://www.politico.com/magazine/story/2016/12/2016-presidential-election-10-moments-trump-clinton-214508.
16. James Hohmann, "The Daily 202: Why Trump Won—and Why the Media Missed It," *Washington Post*, November 9, 2016.
17. Sean Trende, "It Wasn't the Poll That Missed, It Was the Pundits," *RealClearPolitics*, November 12, 2016, http://www.realclearpolitics.com/articles/2016/11/12/it_wasnt_the_polls_that_missed_it_was_the_pundits_132333.html.
18. David Brooks, "No, Not Trump, Not Ever," *New York Times*, March 18, 2016.
19. Margaret Sullivan, "The Media Didn't Want to Believe Trump Could Win. So They Looked the Other Way," *Washington Post*, November 9, 2016.
20. Will Rahn, "Commentary: The Unbearable Smugness of the Press," *CBSNews*, November 10, 2016, http://www.cbsnews.com/news/commentary-the-unbearable-smugness-of-the-press-presidential-election-2016/.
21. Bill Bishop, *The Big Sort: Why the Clustering of Like-Minded America Is Tearing Us Apart* (Boston: Houghton Mifflin Harcourt, 2008).
22. Ibid., 9–10.
23. Ibid., 44.
24. Ibid., 30.
25. Ibid., 11.
26. Paul F. Lazarsfeld and Robert K. Merton, "Friendship as a Social Process: A Substantive and Methodological Analysis," *Freedom and Control in Modern Society* 18, no. 1 (1954): 18–66.
27. Valdis Krebs, "New Political Patterns," *Orgnet*, October 2008, http://www.orgnet.com/divided.html.
28. Watts, *Everything Is Obvious*: *Once You Know the Answer*, 257.
29. Gueorgi Kossinets and Duncan J. Watts, "Origins of Homophily in an Evolving Social Network," *American Journal of Sociology* 115, no. 2 (2009): 405–450.
30. "Planet Money T-shirt," *Kickstarter*, April 30, 2013, https://www.kickstarter.com/projects/planetmoney/planet-money-t-shirt.
31. Farhad Manjoo, "Podcasting Blossoms, but in Slow Motion," *New York Times*, June 17, 2015.

32. Christopher Zinsli, "'This American Life' Producer Raises $1.5 Million for Podcast Startup Gimlet," *Wall Street Journal*, November 11, 2014.
33. Nicholas Quah, "Hot Pod: Panoply's Parent Company Takes a Stake in Gimlet Media," *Nieman Lab*, December 8, 2015, http://www.niemanlab.org/2015/12/hot-pod-panoplys-parent-company-takes-a-stake-in-gimlet-media/.
34. Gimlet, "#19 Diversity Report" (audio podcast), *Startup*, December 17, 2015, https://gimletmedia.com/episode/19-diversity-report/.
35. Ibid.
36. Ibid.
37. Ibid.
38. Ibid.
39. Ibid.

10. Skip Mixers — Share Activities Instead

1. Jon Levy, interview with the author, December 13, 2016.
2. Ibid.
3. Ibid.
4. Ibid.
5. Ibid.
6. Ibid.
7. Chris Schembra, interview with the author, December 15, 2016.
8. Ibid.
9. Ibid.
10. Ibid.
11. Paul Ingram and Michael W. Morris, "Do People Mix at Mixers? Structure, Homophily, and the 'Life of the Party,'" *Administrative Science Quarterly* 52, no. 4 (2007): 566.
12. Brian Uzzi, interview with the author, May 26, 2017.
13. Ibid.
14. Brian Uzzi, "Keys to Understanding Your Social Capital," *Journal of Microfinance/ESR Review* 10, no. 2 (2008): 11.
15. Ed Catmull, "How Pixar Fosters Collective Creativity," *Harvard Business Review* 86, no. 9 (2008): 64.
16. Oliver Franklin-Wallis, "How Pixar Embraces a Crisis," *Wired*, November 17, 2015, http://www.wired.co.uk/article/pixar-embraces-crisis-the-good-dinosaur.
17. Debapratim Purkayastha, "Pixar University: A Distinctive Aspect of Pixar's Organizational Culture and Innovation," Case CLHR017 (Hyperabad, India: ICMR Center for Management Research, 2009).
18. Ed Catmull, with Amy Wallace, *Creativity, Inc.: Overcoming the Unseen Forces That Stand in the Way of True Inspiration* (New York: Random House, 2014), 220.

19. Ibid.
20. Ibid.
21. Ibid.
22. Jessi Hempel, "Pixar University: Thinking Outside the Mouse," *SFGate,* June 4, 2003, http://www.sfgate.com/news/article/Pixar-University-Thinking-Outside-The-Mouse-2611923.php.
23. Catmull, "How Pixar Fosters Collective Creativity," 64.

11. Build Stronger Ties Through Multiplexity

1. Timothy L. O'Brien and Stephanie Saul, "Buffett to Give Bulk of His Fortune to Gates Charity," *New York Times,* June 26, 2006.
2. "Mary Gates, 64; Helped Her Son Start Microsoft," *New York Times,* June 11, 1994.
3. Bill Gates, "25 Years of Learning and Laughing with Warren Buffett," *LinkedIn Pulse,* July 5, 2016, https://www.linkedin.com/pulse/25-years-learning-laughing-warren-buffett-bill-gates.
4. Martha T. Moore, "Billionaires Bank on Bridge to Trump Poker," *USA Today,* December 19, 2005.
5. Susanna Kim, "Berkshire Directors Lowest-Paid of S&P Firms," *ABCNews,* May 31, 2013, http://abcnews.go.com/blogs/business/2013/05/berkshire-directors-lowest-paid-of-sp-firms/.
6. Procter & Gamble, "Our History—How It Began," https://www.pg.com/en_US/downloads/media/Fact_Sheets_CompanyHistory.pdf.
7. J. D. Harrison, "When We Were Small: Ben & Jerry's," *Washington Post,* May 14, 2014.
8. Ibid.
9. Rosanna Greenstreet, "How We Met: Ben Cohen and Jerry Greenfield," *Independent,* May 27, 1995, http://www.independent.co.uk/arts-entertainment/how-we-met-ben-cohen-and-jerry-greenfield-1621559.html.
10. Constance L. Hays, "Ben & Jerry's to Unilever, with Attitude," *New York Times,* April 3, 2000.
11. Kadushin, *Understanding Social Networks: Theories, Concepts, and Findings*.
12. Simone Ferriani, Fabio Fonti, and Raffaele Corrado, "The Social and Economic Bases of Network Multiplexity: Exploring the Emergence of Multiplex Ties," *Strategic Organization* 11, no. 1 (2013): 7–34.
13. Jessica R. Methot, Jeffery A. LePine, Nathan P. Podsakoff, and Jessica Siegel Christian, "Are Workplace Friendships a Mixed Blessing? Exploring Tradeoffs of Multiplex Relationships and Their Associations with Job Performance," *Personnel Psychology* 69, no. 2 (2015): 311–355.
14. Ibid., 339.

15. Rick Aalbers, Wilfred Dolfsma, and Otto Koppius, "Rich Ties and Innovative Knowledge Transfer Within a Firm," *British Journal of Management* 25, no. 4 (2014): 833–848.
16. Ibid., 844.
17. Whitney Johnson, interview with the author, March 29, 2017.
18. Ibid.
19. Clayton M. Christensen, *The Innovator's Dilemma: When New Technologies Cause Great Firms to Fail* (Boston: Harvard Business School Publishing, 1997).
20. Whitney Johnson, interview with the author, March 29, 2017.

Conclusion

1. Nicholas A. Christakis and James H. Fowler, *Connected: The Surprising Power of Our Social Networks and How They Shape Our Lives* (New York: Little, Brown & Co., 2009).
2. Albert-László Barabási, *Bursts: The Hidden Pattern Behind Everything We Do, from Your Email to Bloody Crusades* (New York: Dutton, 2010).
3. Nicholas A. Christakis and James H. Fowler, "The Spread of Obesity in a Large Social Network over 32 Years," *New England Journal of Medicine* 357, no. 4 (2007): 370–379.
4. Nicholas A. Christakis and James H. Fowler, "The Collective Dynamics of Smoking in a Large Social Network," *New England Journal of Medicine* 358, no. 21 (2008): 2249–2258.
5. Christakis and Fowler, *Connected: The Surprising Power of Our Social Networks and How They Shape Our Lives*, 116.
6. James H. Fowler and Nicholas A. Christakis, "Dynamic Spread of Happiness in a Large Social Network: Longitudinal Analysis over 20 Years in the Framingham Heart Study," *BMJ* 337 (2008): a2338.
7. Christakis and Fowler, *Connected: The Surprising Power of Our Social Networks and How They Shape Our Lives*, 51.

Index

About the Author

David Burkus is a best-selling author, a sought-after speaker, and a business school professor.

David is the author of two previous books, *Under New Management* and *The Myths of Creativity*. He is a regular contributor to *Harvard Business Review*, and his work has been featured in *Fast Company*, the *Financial Times*, *Inc.* magazine, *Bloomberg BusinessWeek*, and the *Wall Street Journal* and on *CBS This Morning*. In 2015, he was named one of the emerging thought leaders most likely to shape the future of business by Thinkers50, the world's premier ranking of management thinkers.

David's innovative views on leadership have earned him invitations to speak to leaders from a variety of organizations. He has delivered keynote speeches and workshops for Fortune 500 companies such as Microsoft, Google, and Stryker and for governmental and military leaders at the US Naval Academy and the Naval Postgraduate School. His TED talk has been viewed over 1.7 million times.

When he's not speaking or writing, David is in the classroom. He is associate professor of leadership and innovation at Oral Roberts University, where he was recently named one of the "Top 40 Under 40 Professors Who Inspire." He serves on the advisory board of Fuse Corps, a nonprofit dedicated to making transformative and replicable change in local government.

David lives outside of Tulsa with his wife and their two boys.